T0351509

PORSCHE

UTAH STATE ROUTE 95

INTRO

Der Moment, in dem wir losfahren, ist immer wieder eine kleine Geburt: Man weiß nie, was unterwegs geschehen wird. Ein Abenteuer entfaltet sich. Schön, dass wir das ganz oft haben können, eigentlich jeden Tag. Insgeheim baut sich dabei aber eine Sehnsucht nach dem ultimativen Abenteuer auf. Nach einer Fahrt, die bis ans Ende der Welt gehen könnte. Diese Sehnsucht hat uns für eine neue Ausgabe von CURVES an den Fuß der Rocky Mountains verschlagen, auf der Suche nach einem Beweis für eine verwegene Theorie: Gegensätze ziehen sich an. Sportwagen und der Wilde Westen, lange Geraden in der Wüste und CURVES zum Beispiel. Wie sehr das aber tatsächlich passt, hat uns am Ende wirklich verblüfft. Und dabei ging es nicht um Fahrspaß auf den Passstraßen der Rocky Mountains oder um Kurvensurfen unter dem blauen Himmel der Sierra Nevada, sondern um etwas Tieferes. Um Freiheit. Um das Lebendigsein. Keine Gegensätze weit und breit. Nur Freude.

—

The moment of departure is always like seeing our planet anew: you never know what might happen, what adventures may unfold. It's wonderful that we experience this so often, every day in fact. Secretly, however, a yearning grows for the ultimate adventure. For a trip that could take us to the end of the world. For the latest edition of CURVES, this yearning led us to the foot of the Rocky Mountains in a search for evidence of a daring theory: opposites attract. Sports cars and the Wild West, long straights in the desert and CURVES, for instance. We were truly amazed at just how congruous this turned out to be. And it wasn't just about savoring the pass roads over the Rocky Mountains or surfing through curves under the blue skies of the Sierra Nevada... it went much deeper than that. It was about freedom. About being alive. No contrasts far and wide. Only joy.

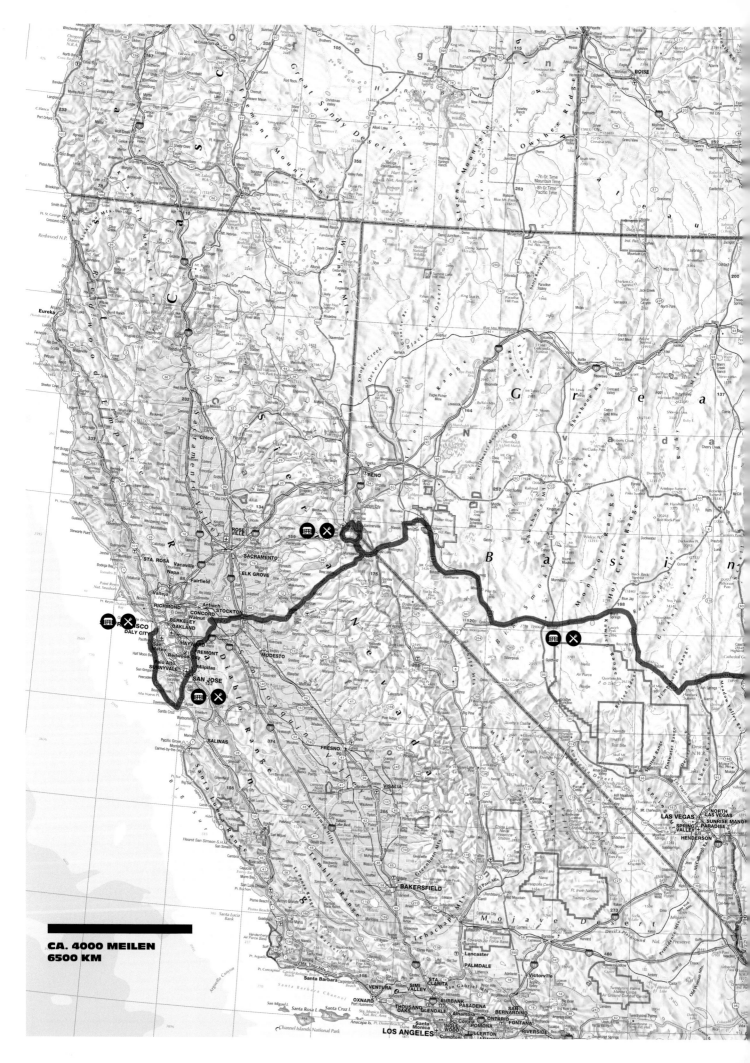

CA. 4000 MEILEN
6500 KM

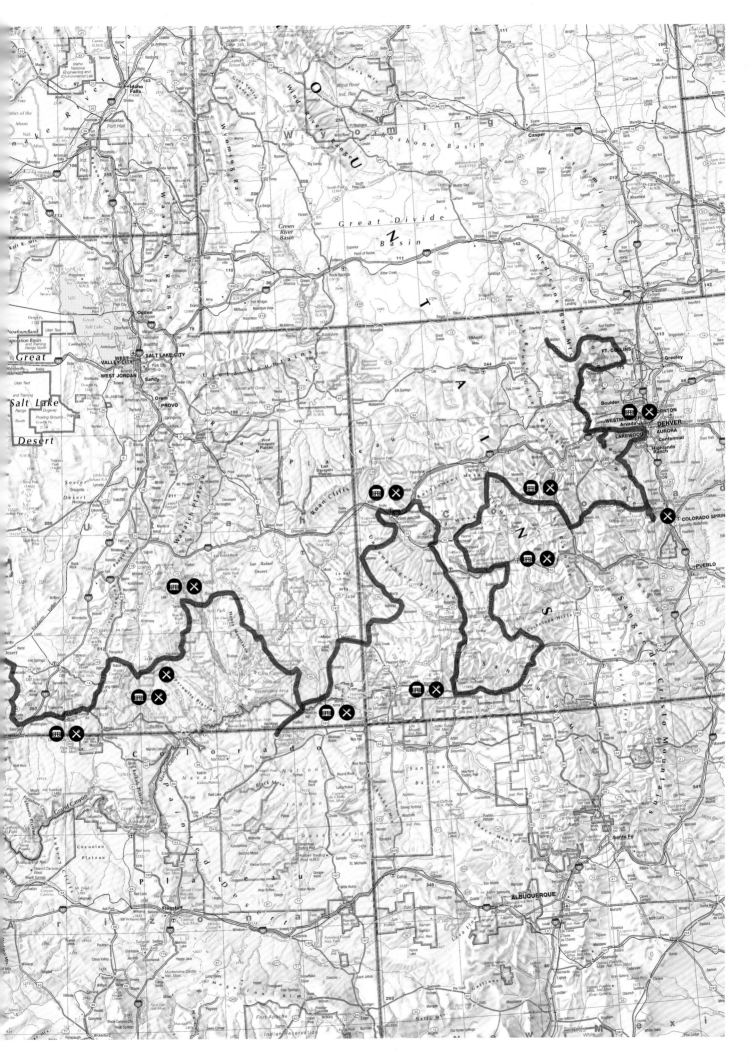

UTAH HIGHWAY 12
SCENIC BYWAY

ETAPPE
STAGE

ETAPPE
STAGE

Über den idealen Startpunkt zur Überquerung der Rocky Mountains lässt sich lang spekulieren. Das Gebirge ist ebenso riesig wie überall sehenswert, am besten nimmt man den Gipfelkamm also mehrfach: Aus Salt Lake City kommend treiben wir deshalb nahe der Grenze zwischen Colorado und Wyoming über den Nordkamm der Rockies, kurven hinter Boulder noch einmal ins Gebirge, verbringen einen Zwischenstopp in der Mile-High-City Denver und dringen dann endlich am Pikes Peak zum östlichsten Punkt unserer Route vor. So gesehen, geht die Überquerung erst hier wirklich los. Auf über 4.000 Metern Höhe, mit Blick auf die großen Ebenen des Mittleren Westens und das weit nach Westen reichende Gebirge. Dramatisch, episch, wild. Dies ist die erste Etappe. Und vor allem nur ein Anfang.

One can spend a lot of time speculating about the ideal starting point to cross the Rocky Mountains. The range is as mighty as it is impressive, so it's best to traverse the range several times: From Salt Lake City, we drift close to the border of Colorado and Wyoming over the North Ridge of the Rockies, then turn into the mountains behind Boulder and stopover at the Mile High City of Denver, before finally heading to Pikes Peak at the easternmost point of our route. In this respect, the crossing really starts here. At an altitude of more than 4,000 meters, overlooking the Great Plains of the Midwest and the mountains that stretch far to the west: dramatic, epic, wild. This is stage one; we've only just begun.

Man könnte die knapp 700 Kilometer lange Strecke von Denver, Colorado, bis zur Kleinstadt Monticello direkt hinter der Grenze zwischen Colorado und dem angrenzenden Bundesstaat Utah über die Interstate 70 in guten sechseinhalb Stunden abhaken, hätte dann ebenfalls den Hauptkamm der Rocky Mountains zur Gänze gequert und ein enormes Stück des Wegs von Denver bis an die Westküste geschafft. Aber überhaupt nicht verstanden, wie hirnzermeißelnd groß die Rocky Mountains sind. Nicht nur Ost-West, sondern auch Nord-Süd. Wie unfassbar vielfältig die Landschaften. Deshalb kreuzen wir in großen Schleifen über das Gebirge: über den Norden bei Aspen nach Carbondale, dann Hotchkiss und Lake City bis beinahe wieder in den Osten des Gebirges bei South Fork, in weitem Bogen bis Durango und erneut nach Norden. Bei Grand Junction machen wir uns auf den Weg nach Südwesten. Und jetzt endlich kennen wir die Rocky Mountains wirklich.

It's possible to cover the 700 or so kilometers from Denver/ Colorado to the town of Monticello, just over the border between Colorado and the neighboring state of Utah via the Interstate 70, in a good six and a half hours, traversing the main ridge of the Rocky Mountains and a huge section of the route from Denver to the west coast. But in doing this, you don't quite grasp the sheer magnitude of the Rocky Mountains – not only from east to west but also north to south – and the unbelievable diversity of the landscapes. For this reason, we cross the mountains in giant loops: via the north near Aspen to Carbondale, then Hotchkiss and Lake City almost to the east of the mountains at South Fork, then a wide sweep to Durango and back to the north. At Grand Junction we head southwest. And only after this do we feel we really know the Rocky Mountains.

ETAPPE
STAGE

ETAPPE
STAGE

Nach den Etappen der Rocky Mountains von Colorado steuern wir auf der dritten Etappe in eine ganz neue Landschaft hinein: Die Canyonlands des US-Bundesstaats Utah sind schroff, magisch und einsam. Den Beginn machen die Streckenabschnitte hinunter zur ehemaligen Uran-Bergbaustadt Bluff. Dann geht es am wilden San Juan River entlang, der mit seinen tief ins Gestein gefrästen Schleifen unglaubliche Landschaften geschaffen hat. Hinter Mexican Hat muss es ein Abstecher ins Monument Valley sein: Die majestätischen Tafelberge in einsamer und endloser Weite sind Fotomotiv Nummer Eins einer Reise durch den Wilden Westen. Ähnlich derbe und trocken zieht sich das Land dem Verlauf des Colorado River entgegen, dann queren wir den Capitol Reef National Park. Bei Hanksville haben wir den nördlichsten Punkt dieser Etappe erreicht und starten nun die Durchquerung der beiden großen Nationalparks rund um das Capitol Reef und das Grand Staircase-Escalante Monument. Vorbei am Bryce Canyon und durch den Zion Nation Park schließen wir diese Fahrt durch Utah ab. Weite Strecken, aber Landschaften wie aus einem Traum.

Die vierte Etappe unserer Durchquerung des Westens der USA könnte bei Freunden gepflegten Kurvensurfens auf den ersten Blick starke Abstoßungsreaktionen auslösen: Quer durch das Große Becken führend, das weite und monotone Innere Nevadas, scheint hier auf gut 530 Meilen für Fahrspaß-Liebhaber kaum etwas zu holen zu sein. Und dieses Urteil muss bis auf wenige Meilen exakt so bestätigt werden. Es sei denn, man schafft den Wechsel zu einer transzendenteren Fortbewegungsweise, die weniger den glorreichen Moment der Kurve anstrebt, als das versunkene Gleiten in einer anderen Welt. Dann findet man hier wirklich eine vollkommen sehens- und fahrenswerte Etappe, die im Nachhinein vielleicht sogar die intensivsten Momente entfaltet: Ab der Grenze von Utah nach Nevada rollen wir geradeaus nach Osten, um bei Crystal Springs auf den Extraterrestrial Highway über Rachel nach Warm Springs abzubiegen. Hier geht es weiter bis nach Tonopah zum Highway 95, dem wir ab Coaldale nach Nordwesten folgen. Über Hawthorne und Yerington fahren wir weiter bis zur 50, ab hier sind es nur noch wenige Meilen nach Carson City. Die Grenze zum US-Bundesstaat California verläuft quer durch den Lake Tahoe – dem Ende der vierten und Start der letzten Etappe.

After the stages through the Rocky Mountains of Colorado, we head into a whole new landscape on leg three: the Canyonlands of the US state of Utah are rugged, magical and lonely. First, the route leads down to the former uranium mining town of Bluff, then along the wild San Juan River, with its loops carved deep into the awe-inspiring landscape. After Mexican Hat, a detour into Monument Valley is a must: the majestic flat-topped butts in an isolated, endless expanse are the number one photo opportunity on a journey through the Wild West. Equally as rugged and dry, the land stretches along the Colorado River; we then cross the Capitol Reef National Park. At Hanksville we reach the northernmost point of this leg and now start to traverse the two large national parks around Capitol Reef and the Grand Staircase-Escalante Monument. Passing Bryce Canyon and through the Zion National Park, we conclude the drive through Utah. It's a long trip, but the landscapes are a dream.

The fourth leg of our traverse of America's West could very well evoke a strong rejection response from friends of sophisticated curve surfing: Crossing the 530 miles of the Great Basin, the wide and monotonous interior of Nevada, doesn't seem to offer a lot for those wanting driving pleasure. And, except for just a few miles, this observation is precisely correct. Unless one manages the transition to a more transcendental mode of travelling that is less about the glorious moment of the curves and more about the rapt glide into another world. Then, you'll discover a truly scenic and drive-worthy stage, which in hindsight offered perhaps even the most intense moments: From the Utah border to Nevada we roll due east, at Crystal Springs taking the Extraterrestrial Highway over Rachel to Warm Springs. From here we continue through Tonopah onto Highway 95, which we follow from Coaldale to the northwest. Passing through Hawthorne and Yerington, we continue to the 50, from here it's just a few miles to Carson City. The border of the US state of California runs straight through Lake Tahoe – the end of the fourth and the start of our final leg.

ETAPPE
STAGE

Auf unserem Weg vom Lake Tahoe zum Pazifik überqueren wir den Hauptkamm der Sierra Nevada auf Höhe des Stanislaus National Forest, landen bei Sonora im Hinterland der großen Küstenebene und machen uns von dort auf den Weg nach San Francisco. Um die Fahrt noch ein letztes Mal auszukosten, versuchen wir die großen Verkehrswege zu meiden und nehmen Nebenstraßen in den Santa Cruz Mountains bis an die Küste. Den Abschluss unserer Fahrt bildet dann die Route über den Highway 1 von Santa Cruz über Half Moon Bay bis San Francisco. Hier kann ein letztes Mal eine Höchstdosis Natur inhaliert werden, der kurze Abschnitt der weltberühmten Küstenstraße ist ideal für den langsamen Entzug nach den riesigen Berg- und Wüstenetappen der letzten Tage.

On our way from Lake Tahoe to the Pacific we cross the main ridge of the Sierra Nevada via the Stanislaus National Forest, ending up near Sonora in the hinterland of the large coastal plain, and make our way from there to San Francisco. To savor the final drive, we try to avoid the major traffic routes and take side roads through the Santa Cruz Mountains to the coast. To conclude our journey we then take Highway 1 from Santa Cruz over Half Moon Bay to San Francisco. Here, for one last time, we inhale a good whiff of nature; the short section of the world famous coastal road is perfect for the slow withdrawal after the mighty mountain and desert stages of the previous day.

EDITORIAL

ES gibt die Blockbuster. Treibende Geschichten mit spektakulärem Handlungsbogen und schillernden Szenen. Mit Momenten, in denen du die Finger tief in den Lehnen des Kinosessels vergraben hast und mit offenem Mund vergisst, weiter Popcorn zu kauen. Und dann sind da die wirklich guten Geschichten. Mit Charakteren, die schmerzhaft echt sind, bitter und komisch zugleich. Voller Tiefgang und unerwarteter Wendungen. Mit Handlungssträngen, die sich langsam entfalten, die man sich erarbeiten muss und die einen danach aber nur umso länger beschäftigen. Geschichten, die etwas mit dir zu tun haben. Auch wenn du das erst im Nachhinein oder unter Tränen entdeckst.

Ein klein wenig ist es so auch mit dieser Fahrt durch den Westen der USA: Üblicherweise stehen New York und Florida, Las Vegas und Kalifornien auf der Bucketlist Weltreisender, diese Orte sind die Blockbuster des Fernwehs. Voller Sonne und Action, voller Aufregung, Pathos und großer Gefühle. Den Zeigefinger hingegen irgendwo zwischen Salt Lake City und den Rocky Mountains auf die Landkarte zu setzen und dort loszufahren, ist nicht gerade eine weit verbreitete Vorgehensweise. Und dabei beginnen genau so die schrägen Geschichten, das wahre Leben. Charakterkino mit schweißtreibendem Story-Telling: Die unfassbar weiten Naturlandschaften des immer noch Wilden Westens müssen aktiv erfahren werden, man kann sie nicht häppchenweise oder als wohlsortierte Attraktionen verpackt erleben. Anderswo gehst du ein paar Stunden lang auf geführte Tour und hast dann die Häuser der Stars gesehen – hier nicht. Anderswo ist die Welt klimatisiert, asphaltiert und mit Wi-Fi ausgestattet – hier nicht. Anderswo gibt es Instant-Gefühle und Ansonsten-Geldzurück-Garantie – hier nicht. Man muss die epische Landschaft wirken lassen, eine Antenne für ihre Geschichten entwickeln, sie vor allem Meile für Meile erleben und als die eigentliche Attraktion empfinden. Das ist zu anstrengend und langweilig für unsere

There are the blockbusters. Powerful stories with spectacular plots and gripping scenes. With moments where you dig your fingernails deep into the armrest of the cinema chair and, with mouth gaping, forget to chew your popcorn. And then there are just really good stories, with characters that are heartrendingly real, bitter and comical in equal parts. With depth and unexpected twists. With narratives that unfold slowly, ones that make you think and keep you thinking for a long time afterwards. Stories that somehow have something to do with you. Even if you only realize this in hindsight. Or in tears.

In some ways, it's the same as our trip through America's West. It's usually New York and Florida, Las Vegas and California on the bucket lists of world travelers – these are the blockbusters of wanderlust. Full of sunshine and action, packed with excitement, pathos and big emotions. But putting your finger on a map between Salt Lake City and the Rocky Mountains and making that your starting point is not exactly a run-of-the-mill travel plan. And this is precisely how unusual stories, real life begins. Character movies with sweat-inducing storytelling: the inconceivably vast natural landscapes of the (still) Wild West have to be encountered firsthand. You can't experience them bit by bit or as nicely-ordered attractions. Elsewhere, you go on a guided tour for a couple of hours and you're shown the homes of the stars – not here. Elsewhere, the world is air-conditioned, paved, and connected to Wi-Fi – not here. Elsewhere, there's instant gratification with a money back guarantee – not here. You have to allow these epic landscapes time to take effect, develop an antenna for their stories, be truly mindful of every single mile and appreciate them as the real attraction. But this might prove too exhausting and boring for our fast-paced, fast-food, pop culture. Here, there are no abrupt cuts or dramaturgy jumps, no special effects or abridged versions. This tour through the mighty, harsh West of the United States is definite-

schnelle Reize gewohnte Fast-Food- und Popkultur. Hier gibt es keine harten Schnitte und keine Dramaturgie-Sprünge, weder Special Effects noch gekürzte Fassungen. Dabei handelt es sich mit dieser Tour durch den großen, herben Westen der USA um einen absoluten Geheimtipp. Wer magische Landschaften erleben möchte, wird die in Colorado, Utah und Nevada finden. Weites, kaum domestiziertes Land und großartige Natur. Hier bückt sich das Land noch nicht unter der Knute einer alles überziehenden Industrie-Landwirtschaft, wie in den Staaten des Mittleren Westens. Hier ist die Witterung zu herb, die Welt zu felsig und schroff, um mit gleichmäßig wogenden Mais-, Getreide- oder Sojafeldern Fuß fassen zu können. Hier finden große Rinderherden, die sich unaufhörlich in Steaks und Hamburger verwandeln können, weder genug Futter noch ein Zuhause.

Unverfälschte Natur spielt zwischen Rocky Mountains und Sierra Nevada daher immer noch eine oscarverdächtige Hauptrolle. Die Rolle des Menschen ist allerdings zwiespältig. Einerseits hat man keine Mühen gescheut, dem Land und seinen Bodenschätzen auf den Pelz zu rücken. Mit welchem Einfallsreichtum und mit welch grober Brutalität dabei agiert wurde, ist immer wieder zu bestaunen. Minen und Bergwerke, rauer Natur abgetrotzte Siedlungen, waghalsig geführte Straßen oder Bahntrassen, in Truppenübungsplätze und Ski-Arenen verwandelte Gegenden – das gehört unverrückbar zum Westen. Andererseits ist dieses Land aber auch zu weit und abgelegen, zu stark und schroff, um selbst in der rücksichtslosesten Kosten-Nutzen-Kalkulation nachhaltig schwarze Zahlen zu schreiben. Der Westen hat es immer wieder geschafft, den Menschen abzuschütteln, auszuhungern und auszusitzen. Genau das hat einen anderen, erfreulicheren Zug der Menschen hervorgeholt: Respekt, großen Stolz auf dieses unbeugsame Land und tiefe Freude an der Natur. Die Beziehung der Menschen zu Land und Natur ist dabei geprägt von sportlicher Entdeckerfreude und einer kämpferischen Go-Anywhere-Attitude. Man möchte nicht in stiller Kontemplation vor Naturwundern erschauern, sondern Berge besteigen, Wüsten durchqueren, Flüsse durchschwimmen. Das mag dem introvertierten Schmetterlingsforscher mit seinem schüchtern geschwungenen Kescher alles zu wild und martialisch sein, aber vielleicht hat gerade dieser zupackende Outdoor-Geist dazu beigetragen, dass viele US-Amerikaner eine intensiv gelebte Beziehung zur Natur pflegen

Üblicherweise stehen New York und Florida, Las Vegas und Kalifornien auf der Bucketlist Weltreisender, diese Orte sind die Blockbuster des Fernwehs.

It's usually New York and Florida, Las Vegas and California on the bucket lists of world travelers – these are the blockbusters of wanderlust.

ly an insider tip. Those who yearn for magical landscapes will find them in Colorado, Utah and Nevada. Vast, barely domesticated land and breathtaking nature. Here, the country has not yet succumbed to wholesale industrial agriculture like in the states of the Midwest. Here, the weather is too harsh, the earth too rocky and rugged, for row upon precisely-spaced row of corn, grain or soy fields to gain a foothold. Here, large herds of cattle, which roll off the assembly line in the form of steaks and hamburgers, find neither enough food nor a home.

The pristine nature between the Rocky Mountains and the Sierra Nevada still plays an Oscar-worthy lead role. However, the role of the human is ambiguous. On the one hand, no effort has been spared in exploiting the country and its mineral resources. One can only gape in astonishment at the audacity and the sheer brutality with which this was done. Quarries and mines, settlements chiseled into inhospitable nature, daring roads or train tracks, terrain converted into military training areas and ski fields – these all belong irrevocably to the West. On the other hand, this land is too isolated and remote, too arid and rugged, to remain in the black figures, even using the most ruthless cost-benefit calculation. The West has always managed to stave off, starve and shut out people. And it is exactly this that has given rise to another more pleasant side of humanity: respect, immense pride for this indomitable land and profound pleasure in its nature. The peoples relationship to this land and nature, is closely linked to the joy of playful discovery and a steadfast "go-anywhere" attitude. They don't want to sit and tremble in quiet contemplation of the natural wonders; they'd rather climb mountains, cross deserts, swim rivers. This may be too wild and martial for the shy butterfly collector with his net swinging timidly, but perhaps this gung-ho outdoor spirit has helped

statt nur intellektueller Theorie zu frönen. Wer Natur als kämpferisches Gegenüber erleben kann und nicht als abstraktes, schutzbedürftiges Elfenwesen, gerät auch nicht in Gefahr, den Kontakt zur Natur zu verlieren. Dass da gejagt, gefischt und geschossen wird, Camping, Biking und Hiking eine bodenständig-säkulare Dreifaltigkeit bilden, mag europäische Vorstellungen von Naturschutz eher verstören. Aber es ist eben so: Anders als im dicht besiedelten Europa mit seinen Kulturlandschaften, gelten in den USA unberührte Naturräume nicht als Ausnahme-Erscheinung. Hier gibt es Platz im Überfluss. Obendrein ist die US-Outdoor-Kultur hart im Geben und Nehmen: Hier wird ein Grizzly, der unvorsichtige Wanderer anfällt, nicht gleich von Polizei oder Armee als Problembär betrachtet, sondern er darf das. Er ist einfach ein ganz normaler Bär. Und die wehren sich eben gegen Menschen, die ihnen und ihren Jungen zu nahe kommen. Du hättest ja nicht ins Revier der Bären gehen müssen. Dein Pech. Oder du hättest deine Flinte dabeihaben können. Pech für den Bären ...

CAPITOL REEF

Ausdruck dieser mit offenem Visier geführten Auseinandersetzung des Menschen mit der Natur sind die Nationalparks. Sie sind zahllos, sie sind wunderschön und sie sind für uns ein Stück weit das Beste der USA. Mehr als vieles andere repräsentieren sie den Geist der Freiheit dieses Landes, hier finden Entdeckergeister noch Nahrung, hier geht es nach jedem Horizont einfach weiter. Dass wir uns mit diesem CURVES auf eine Reise durch den Wilden Westen der USA gemacht haben, liegt also ausnahmsweise zuerst an dieser unermesslich weiten Landschaft und ihrer herrlich vielfältigen, magischen Natur. Auf der Fahrt von Denver nach San Francisco gehen einem die beinahe transzendenten Momente nie aus. Dieses Land macht froh und sprachlos. Wie tiefgreifend und überwältigend das ist, zeigt die Tatsache, dass wir die Straße und ihre Kurven erst an Platz zwei unserer Highlights setzen: In jeder anderen Ecke der Welt würden die Bergstraßen und Pässe der Rockies und der Sierra Nevada satte 11 von möglichen 10 Punkten bekommen – hier sind sie Nebendarsteller. Und selbst das ist ein Grund, lieber nach Walden, Colorado, oder Rachel, Nevada, zu fahren, statt nach Las Vegas oder Miami. Wenn Sie dort waren, wissen Sie, was gemeint ist.

many Americans maintain a lively relationship with nature rather than simply indulging in intellectual theory. Anyone who can experience nature as a formidable opponent rather than as an abstract elflike creature in need of protection will not be in danger of losing contact to nature. The fact that huntin', shootin', fishin', and camping, biking, and hiking form down-home earthly trinities may upset the European notion of conservation.

But that's just how it is: Unlike in densely-populated Europe with its cultural landscapes, the untouched natural spaces in the US are not considered exceptional. There is so much space here. On top of that, the US outdoor culture is tough in giving and taking: Here, it's okay for a grizzly to attack a hapless hiker without immediately being considered a 'problem' bear by the police or armed forces. It's just part of being a bear. And bears defend themselves when people get too close to them or their cubs. It's your fault for venturing into bear territory. Bad luck for you. You could have taken a rifle with you. Bad luck for the bear...

The true expression of this open-minded conflict between man and nature are the national parks. They are many, and they are glorious. For us, they are somehow the best of the USA. More than anything else, the national parks represent the country's spirit of freedom; here explorers still get their fill, here adventure continues far beyond the horizon. The fact that we took CURVES on a journey through the Wild West of the USA is, first and foremost, because of the vast landscape and its wonderfully diverse, magical natural environment. On the drive from Denver to San Francisco, the almost transcendent moments never stopped. This land leaves you happy and speechless. How profound and overwhelming it is, is evident in the fact that the road and the curves came second on the list of highlights: In every other corner of the world, the mountain roads and passes of the Rockies and the Sierra Nevada would have received a whopping 11 out of a possible 10 points – here they are the supporting actors. And this alone is reason enough to choose to drive to Walden, Colorado, or Rachel, Nevada, instead of Las Vegas or Miami. If you go there, you'll understand why.

PIKES PEAK

RIMROCK DRIVE

COLORADO STATE
HIGHWAY 141

MOUNT EVANS

SAN JUAN SKYWAY
SCENIC BYWAY

MONUMENT VALLEY

UTAH STATE ROAD 95

BRYCE CANYON

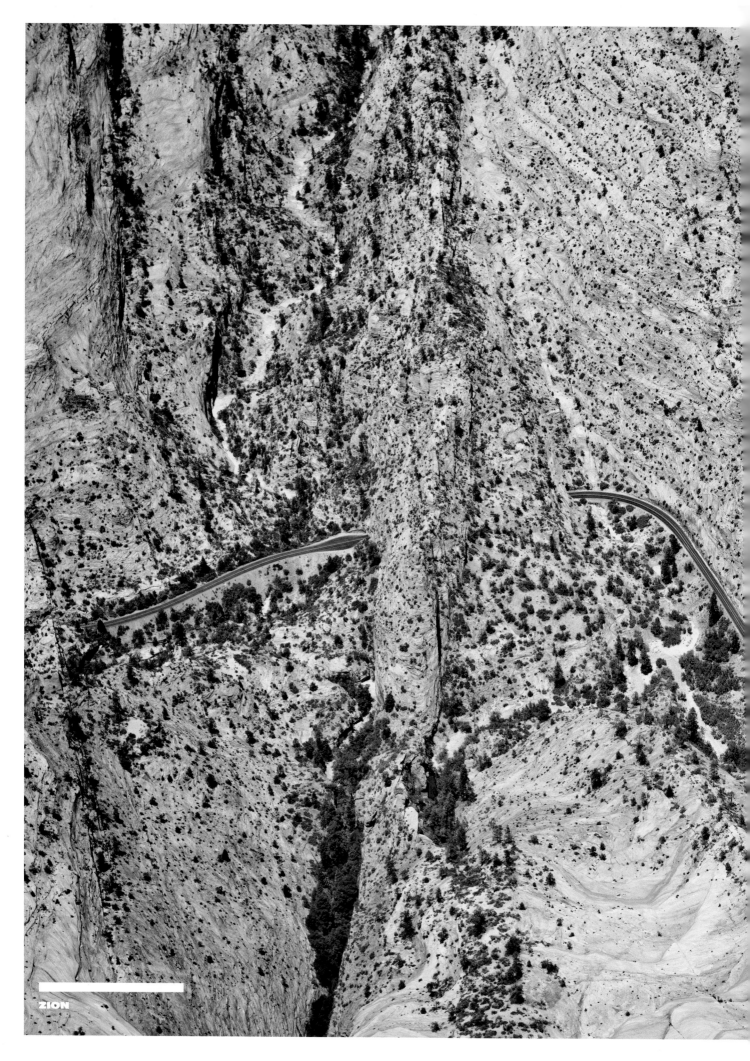

ZION

SNOW CANYON
STATE PARK

HIGHWAY 101

SAN FRANCISCO

WALDEN PIKES PEAK

700 KM • 11 STUNDEN // 435 MILES • 11 HOURS

Es ist so weit. Genau jetzt könnte ein staatstragendes Zitat gut passen. Der Mufflon-Kopf an der Blockhüttenwand gegenüber scheint gespannt zu warten. Starrt dich aus obsidianglasschwarzen Augäpfeln konzentriert an. Auch die Büste eines mächtigen Rothirschs schielt bedeutungsvoll in deine Richtung und schmettert einen lautlosen Brunftschrei ins Restaurant.

—

The time has come. A profound quote would be fitting at this point. The head of a wild bighorn sheep on the opposite wall of the log cabin seems to be waiting in suspense. It fixes you with its beady, black glass eyes. The wall-mounted mighty red deer also stares expectantly in your direction, a silent rutting call roars through the restaurant.

Also gut, Walden, Colorado: „Jedem Anfang wohnt ein Zauber inne!" – Wie ein Mantra hängen die Worte im leeren Frühstücksraum des River Rock Café, du nickst Mufflon und Hirsch zu – und machst dich endlich zufrieden grinsend über einen mächtigen Breakfast-Burrito her. Der Bedeutsamkeit des Augenblicks wäre mit diesem Moment voller Besinnlichkeit ausreichend Genüge getan. Jetzt darf das Leben wieder weitergehen. Draußen wummern gut eingetragene Pickup-Trucks über die Main Street zwischen Mountain View Baptist Church und Jack's Auto Parts, verröcheln für eine Besorgung vor dem Country Store oder bei Family Dollar. Am Horizont tragen Viertausender fleckige Sommer-Schneehauben unter königsblauem Himmel und vielsagende Namen wie Lulu Mountain oder Desolation Peak. Trostlos ist hier aber überhaupt nichts, denn heute geht sie los, unsere große Tour über die Rockies. Zuerst von West nach Ost, dann von Nord nach Süd, weiter den ganzen langen Weg über die Berge zurück und immer weiter nach Westen, und jede Meile wird wunderbar. Ganz bestimmt.

Dass wir die Startlinie ausgerechnet in Walden, Colorado ziehen, hat genau einen Grund: Es passt gut. Zwischen Salt Lake City und Denver gelegen, im Norden der Rocky Mountains, kreuzen sich hier in der Mitte des North Park zwei stille Highways. Du kommst also hin und du kommst wieder weg. Das ist übrigens die Essenz vieler Orte im Westen. Und ein ganz klein wenig auch die Essenz des Unterwegsseins im CURVES-Stil. Tief in unserer Seele zieht Tumbleweed dahin, getrieben von einem endlosen Wind über offener Weite. Wir nennen es „soulful driving", wischen deshalb jetzt die fettigen Finger an einer dünnen Papierserviette ab, schieben ein paar Dollarnoten unter die große Kaffeetasse

Okay, Walden, Colorado: "There's magic in every new beginning!" These words hang like a mantra in the empty breakfast room of the River Rock Café. You nod to the bighorn and the buck and, with a satisfied grin, tuck in to the massive breakfast burrito. This moment of reflection would have done justice to the importance of the situation. Now, life can go on. Outside, well-worn pick-up trucks growl down Main Street between the Mountain View Baptist Church and Jack's Auto Parts, coming to a shuddery stop outside the Country Store or the Family Dollar store. On the horizon, four-thousander peaks with evocative names like Lulu Mountain and Desolation Peak wear patchy summer snow caps under a royal blue sky. Nothing is desolate here, because today it starts: our big journey over the Rockies. First from west to east, then from north to south, continuing all the way back over the mountains and on to the west, where every mile will be wonderful. For sure.

There's a very good reason for starting in Walden, Colorado: it simply works. Here, between Salt Lake City and Denver in the north of the Rocky Mountains, two lonely highways intersect in the middle of North Park. So you arrive and you leave again. Actually, this is the essence of many places in the West and, in some small way, also the essence of being on the road, CURVES style. Deep in our souls tumbleweeds roll, pushed along by an endless wind over a wide, open expanse. We call it 'soulful driving'; we wipe our greasy fingers on a thin paper serviette, shove a couple of dollar bills under the big coffee mug, and march out onto the street.

Stop for a moment, straighten the sunglasses, prick up the ears. Is that the faint strains of a harmonica drifting on the

und marschieren auf die Straße hinaus. Kurz stehen bleiben, Sonnenbrille zurechtrücken, in den Wind lauschen. Spielt da nicht irgendwo klagend eine Mundharmonika? Nee, verhört. Deshalb hinters Haus und dort wartet im Schatten auf einem Kiesplatz unser Auto. Silbern. Kühl. Muskelbepackt.

Raus auf die Straße, die Nase des Wagens fängt Sonnenlicht ein. Dieses ätherische, eiskalte Leuchten eines Präriemorgens auf 2500 Metern Höhe, das schimmernd über den Lack fließt, als wäre es eine Brise aus hellgoldenem Samt. Jetzt mit knurrendem Motor die Straße hinunter. Unsere schlanke Sport-Maschine wirkt im Land der Offroad-Boliden und automobilen Nutzwert-Geräte wie ein Fremdkörper. Aber sie kickt entschlossen Rollsplit und Staub zur Seite, schnürt zum Ortsausgang nach Südosten und dann rauf auf den State Highway 14. Der zieht in langgezogenen Bögen durchs weite Tal, wird von struppiger Buschlandschaft, kleinen Birken und hageren Kiefern begleitet. In Sichtweite stolpert der Michigan River nebenher. Ein schmales Rinnsal, aus den Bergen kommend, auf einer kurzen Reise zum North Platte River unterwegs. Hey, nimm uns mit, Junge!

Vorbei an Gould, einer kleinen Ansammlung von Blockhütten, dann weiter ins Gebirge hinauf. Die Straße nimmt sich jetzt ganz ernst, muss sie auch: Das zufällige Dahinschlendern ist vorbei, jetzt stellen sich ihr echte Berge in den Weg. Grober, zerfurchter und welliger Asphalt war einmal, jetzt wirkt die Straße auf ihrer Trasse ganz konzentriert und energisch, selbst der gelbe Mittelstrich scheint mit Lineal und Zirkel gezogen zu sein. Die Strecke ist in die Flanken des Tals gefräst, läuft beeindruckend zielstrebig dahin. Mit weiten Bögen geht es nach Osten, dann in großem Schwenk nordwärts. Nadelbäume stehen in Rudeln stramm senkrecht, als wären es

wind? No, must have misheard. Behind the building, our car waits on the gravel in the shade. Silver. Cool. Muscular. Pulling onto the road, the nose of the car catches the sun's rays. This ethereal, icy cold glow of a prairie morning at 2,500 meters, shimmering over the paint as if it were a breeze of golden velvet. Down the street now with the engine thrumming; in the land of off-roaders and utility vehicles, our slender sports car looks out of place. Still, it resolutely spits gravel and dust to the side, glides out of town to the southeast and onto State Highway 14, taking long, sweeping arcs through the wide valley, through scrubby bushland, stunted birches and tortured pines. Within view, the Michigan River tumbles along next to the road. A small trickle coming from the mountain on its short journey to the nearby North Platte River. Hey, man, take us with you!

Past Gould, a small cluster of log cabins, then up into the mountains. The road gets serious now, and so it should: The easy stroll is over, now the real mountains tower in the way. The coarse, rutted, bumpy asphalt now gives way to a concentrated, assertive surface; even the yellow center line seems to have been drawn with ruler and compass. The route carves into the slopes of the valley, forging ahead with impressive purpose. We head east in broad sweeps before veering north with a wide swing.

Conifers stand at attention in groups, as if they were iron filings in a vertical magnetic field. Past reservoir lakes, over the first mountain ridge and then down the northern flank into a narrow valley where birch and ash trees seem to sway to the rhythm of a country song; silver leaves aflutter. Overhead, spruce trees cling to rugged, rocky cliffs. And so it goes, mile after mile. The Michigan River has left us, of course, on the other side of the mountain.

HOTELS

THE RAMBLE HOTEL
1280 25TH STREET
DENVER, CO 80205
RESERVATIONS: (720) 996 - 6300
WWW.THERAMBLEHOTEL.COM

MOUNT EVANS

MOUNT EVANS

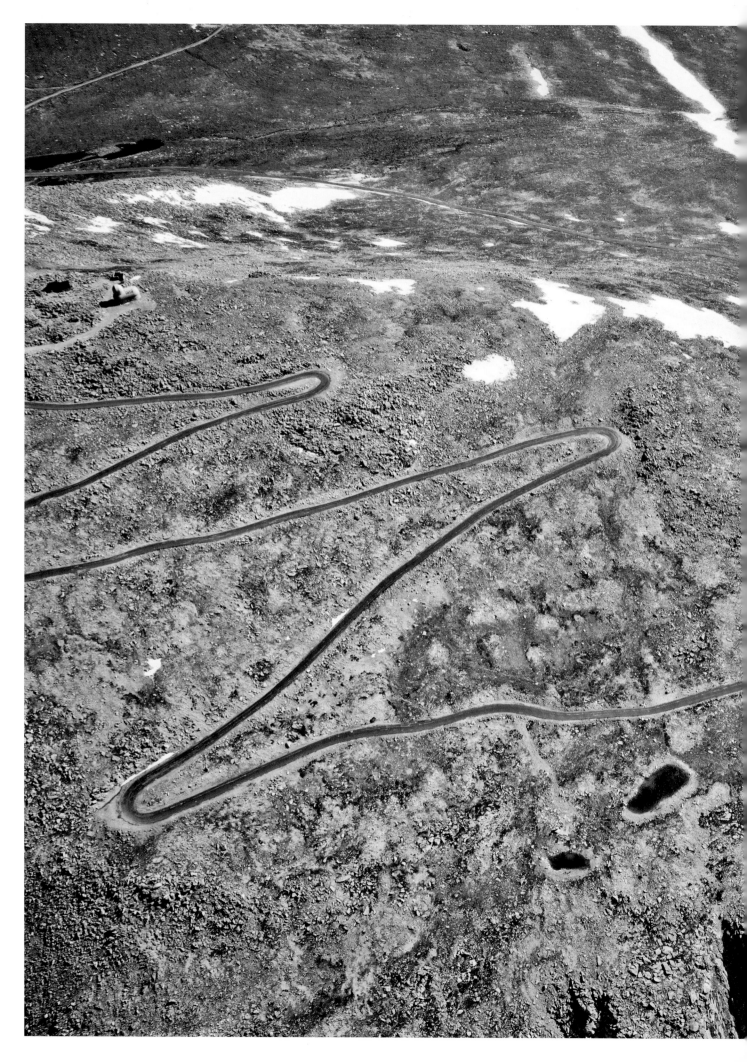

MOUNT EVANS

Eisenspäne in einem vertikal laufenden Magnetfeld. Vorbei an Stauseen, über den ersten Berggrat und dann auf der Nordseite hinunter in ein enges Tal, in dem Birken und Eschen mit silbrig wirbelnden Blättern im Rhythmus eines Country-Songs wirbeln, während sich weiter oben Fichten an schroffe, felsige Hänge klammern.
So geht das Meile um Meile um Meile, der Michigan River hat uns selbstverständlich auf der anderen Bergseite verlassen. Wir haben einen neuen Gesellen, den Cache la Poudre River, der seinen Namen in den Tagen des alten Westens von französischen Trappern bekommen hat und bei genauem Hinhören tatsächlich einen weichen Akzent spricht, während er durch sein steiniges Bett strudelt. Es geht durch felsiges Terrain, die Straße schneidet in tiefe Canyons, kurvt dann in immer weiter werdende Täler und landet schließlich nach vielen Meilen auf dem Highway 287, der in vier Spuren hinunter nach Denver zieht. Wir nehmen eine Abkürzung - die Stove Prairie Road 27, die sich als Traumstraße herausstellt. Und dann der Umweg durch die Berge. Die 34 nach Westen, gegen erste Höhen anbrandend, dann Kurven. Endlich wieder Kurven. Estes Park. 12.000 feet. Hammer. Unterhalb des Deer Mountain und am Sundance Mountain vorbei, dann nach Süden und zum Lake Granby, der mit seinen Segelbooten zwischen verschneiten Berggipfeln aussieht wie eine Mischung aus Schweden und Schweiz. Déjà-vu für uns Rolling Stones aus der Alten Welt.

Weiter über die US-40, die hinter Fraser endlich in eleganten Serpentinen zurück nach Osten surft und dann auf den Interstate Highway 70 trifft, die große Ost-West-Achse. Als Schmankerl nehmen wir noch den Mount Evans mit. Atem(be)raubend. Mit 4.348 Metern ist er der höchste anfahrbare Punkt Nordamerikas. Uns bleibt nach

We now have a new companion, the Cache la Poudre River, which got its name from French trappers in the days of the old West and, if you listen closely, actually speaks a soft accent as it trips and spills over its stony bed. Onward through rocky terrain, the road cuts into deep canyons, then curves in ever-broadening valleys to finally end up after many miles on Highway 287, which leads down into Denver on four lanes. We take a shortcut, the Stove Prairie Road 27 – a dream road as it turns out – then a detour through the mountains: the US-34 West, set against the crests of the first mountains, then curves.

At last, more curves. Estes Park. 12,000 feet. Awesome. Passing under Deer Mountain and Sundance Mountain, to Lake Granby in the south, which looks like a combination of Sweden and Switzerland with its sailboats between snow-capped peaks. Déjà-vu for us Rolling Stones from the Old World. We continue on the US-40. After Fraser, the road surfs in elegant serpentines back to the east and then joins up with the Interstate Highway 70; the great east-west transcontinental junction. As a special treat, we tackle Mount Evans. Breathtaking... literally. At 4,348 meters in altitude, it is North America's highest drivable point. After the long sweep through the mountain range to the west of Boulder, our only choice is to return to the plains – we have a date with Pikes Peak, the big mountain south of Denver. However, as we reach Golden and the first suburbs, it becomes clear that we'll not drive many more miles on this day.

Thunderclouds boil to the stratosphere over the Great Plains in the east. The air in the city is scorching and eerily still. As if hypnotized, we roll straight on and don't quite manage to stop. Continuing to the

RESTAURANT

WESTBOUND &
DOWN BREWING COMPANY
1617 MINER STREET
IDAHO SPRINGS
PHONE: (720) 502-3121
WWW.WESTBOUNDANDDOWN.COM

dem weiten Bogen durch die Gebirgskette im Westen von Boulder doch wieder nur der Weg zurück in die Ebene, denn wir haben einen Termin am Pikes Peak, dem großen Berg im Süden von Denver. Als wir aber bei Golden in den ersten Vororten landen, wird klar, dass wir an diesem Tag nicht mehr viele Meilen fahren werden. Gewitterwolken haben sich über den großen Ebenen im Osten bis an die Stratosphäre getürmt, brütende Hitze und gespenstische Windstille herrschen in der Stadt. Wie hypnotisiert rollen wir geradeaus und schaffen es einfach nicht, die Bahn zu verlassen. Immer weiter nach Osten durch die Stadt, magisch angezogen von einem fast schwarz werdenden Himmel. An der Zufahrt zum Rocky Mountain Arsenal, dem Naturpark zwischen Flughafen und South Platte River, ziehen wir von der Interstate und rollen in die Grasebene hinein. Trockene Steppe, darüber ein bleischwerer Himmel, in dem Blitze zucken. Dann kommen sie, die ersten heißen Windböen. Die Luft duftet nach Hitze und trockenem Gras, nach Wildheit und Gefahr. Tornadoröhren saugen Staub in scharfen Strudeln zwanzig, dreißig Meter in die Höhe und zerstieben im nächsten Moment kollabierend. Eine Herde Bisons steht stoisch unbewegt neben der Straße, nur die langen Bärte der buckligen Ungetüme wehen im Wind. Das Auto rollt aus. Bleibt stehen. Wir warten mit klopfendem Herzen, sehen die Regenfront im Eiltempo heranziehen. Gischtende Wassermassen, die aus Nachtschwärze auf die Prärie herunterstürzen. Dann hat uns der Regen erreicht. Peitscht in ersten dicken Tropfen auf das Autodach, trommelt, flutet, rauscht. Minutenlanger Vollwaschgang, ohne auch nur ein paar Schritte weit sehen zu können.

Irgendwann lässt die Sintflut nach und verwandelt sich in einen stetigen Regen, langsam bekommt der Himmel wieder Struktur. Wir wenden den Wagen und

east through the city, magically drawn to the bruised and brooding sky. At the entrance to the Rocky Mountain Arsenal, the national park between the airport and the South Platte River, we leave the Interstate and continue through grassy plains. Dry prairie, above it a leaden sky shot through with bolts of lightning. The first hot gusts hit. The air smells of heat and dry grass, of tempest and danger. Dust devils form, sucking up debris in thin swirls, twenty, thirty meters high, only to dissipate moments later. A herd of bison stands stoically still beside the road, only the matted beards of the humpbacked giants waving in the wind. The car pulls to the side of the road and stops. We wait with quickened pulse, watching as the rain squalls approach.

A curtain of torrential water beats down from the inky sky onto the prairie. The rain reaches us. The first fat drops pelt the roof of our car; drumming, drenching, deafening. Minutes on heavy duty wash cycle, visibility almost zero. Eventually the deluge subsides and turns into a steady rain, gradually shapes take form again. We turn around and scud back towards the towering skyscrapers. A mountainous landscape of concrete and glass huddles against the silhouette of the Rockies and we suddenly develop an appetite to explore. In the city, streets are submerged, cars punt through ankle-deep puddles, until suddenly the clouds clear and the stars twinkle between the skyscrapers.

The next morning, blue skies shine over the city, a steady wind brings fresh, cool air. We hit the road again. Denver slowly disappears behind us and, with it, the endless sea of grass of the Great Plains, which stretches for hundreds of kilometers to the east behind the city. We take Highway 285 at Indian Hills, heading southwest, then cross Pine Valley to the south, switching

DINER

MILDRED'S CAFE
4645 FOUNTAIN AVE,
CASCADE, CO 80809
WWW.MILDREDS-CAFE.COM

MOUNT EVANS

Wir haben gehört, dass im normalen Touristenverkehr auf der extrem hoch liegenden Bergstraße Fahrspaß kaum eine Rolle spielen soll. Das Tempo ist streng limitiert und Überholversuche verpönt. Es gilt also früh am Berg zu sein, als Erster am Kassenhaus der Mautstrecke. Und dann entspannt zum Gipfel surfen. Vollgas im Herzen.

fegen die Straße zurück in Richtung der aufragenden Wolkenkratzer. Ein Gebirge aus Beton und Glas drängt sich vor der Silhouette der Rockies und wir haben plötzlich große Lust, uns auch hier umzusehen. In der Stadt stehen ganze Straßenzüge unter Wasser, das Auto gischtet durch knöcheltiefe Pfützen, bis sich plötzlich die Wolken verziehen und die Sterne zwischen den Wolkenkratzern leuchten.

Am nächsten Morgen strahlt blauer Himmel über der Stadt, ein konstanter Wind bringt frische, kühle Luft heran. Wir sind wieder unterwegs. Langsam verschwindet Denver hinter uns und auch das endlose Grasmeer der Great Plains, das hinter der Stadt Hunderte von Kilometern nach Osten reicht. Wir treiben das Auto bei Indian Hills auf den Highway 285, Kurs Südwest, kreuzen dann durch das Pine Valley nach Süden, wechseln bei Deckers auf die 67 und haben nach 150 Kilometern Cascade erreicht. Ausgangspunkt für den Sturm zum Gipfel des Pikes Peak. Der ragt 4300 Meter hoch in den Himmel und wehrt sich jedes Jahr nach Leibeskräften gegen den Ansturm der Racer des berühmten Hillclimb. Wir haben gehört, dass im normalen Touristenverkehr auf der extrem hoch liegenden Bergstraße Fahrspaß kaum eine Rolle spielen soll. Das Tempo ist streng limitiert und Überholversuche verpönt. Es gilt also früh am Berg zu sein, als Erster am Kassenhaus der Mautstrecke. Und dann entspannt zum Gipfel surfen. Vollgas im Herzen. Hier und heute muss das reichen.

We've heard that it's not a lot of fun in normal tourist traffic to drive the extremely high mountain road. The speed is strictly limited and overtaking attempts are frowned upon. Hence, it pays to get up the mountain early, to be the first at the toll booth. Then enjoy a relaxed 'surf' up the mountain. Full throttle, but only in spirit.

to the 67 at Deckers before finally reaching Cascade 150 kilometers later: the starting point for our conquest of the Pikes Peak summit. The mountain towers 4,300 meters into the sky, defending itself valiantly every year against the onslaught of racers tackling the famous hill climb.

We've heard that it's not a lot of fun in normal tourist traffic to drive the extremely high mountain road. The speed is strictly limited and overtaking attempts are frowned upon. Hence, it pays to get up the mountain early, to be the first at the toll booth. Then enjoy a relaxed 'surf' up the mountain. Full throttle, but only in spirit. Right here and now, this has to do.

WALDEN PIKES PEAK

Über den idealen Startpunkt zur Überquerung der Rocky Mountains lässt sich lang spekulieren. Das Gebirge ist ebenso riesig wie überall sehenswert, am besten nimmt man den Gipfelkamm also mehrfach: Aus Salt Lake City kommend treiben wir deshalb nahe der Grenze zwischen Colorado und Wyoming über den Nordkamm der Rockies, kurven hinter Boulder noch einmal ins Gebirge, verbringen einen Zwischenstopp in der Mile-High-City Denver und dringen dann endlich am Pikes Peak zum östlichsten Punkt unserer Route vor. So gesehen, geht die Überquerung erst hier wirklich los. Auf über 4.000 Metern Höhe, mit Blick auf die großen Ebenen des Mittleren Westens und das weit nach Westen reichende Gebirge. Dramatisch, episch, wild. Dies ist die erste Etappe. Und vor allem nur ein Anfang.

—

One can spend a lot of time speculating about the ideal starting point to cross the Rocky Mountains. The range is as mighty as it is impressive, so it's best to traverse the range several times: From Salt Lake City, we drift close to the border of Colorado and Wyoming over the North Ridge of the Rockies, then turn into the mountains behind Boulder and stopover at the Mile High City of Denver, before finally heading to Pikes Peak at the easternmost point of our route. In this respect, the crossing really starts here. At an altitude of more than 4,000 meters, overlooking the Great Plains of the Midwest and the mountains that stretch far to the west: dramatic, epic, wild. This is stage one; we've only just begun.

700 KM • 11 STUNDEN // 435 MILES • 11 HOURS

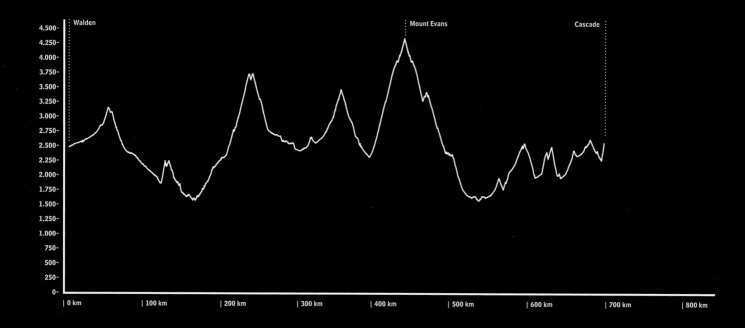

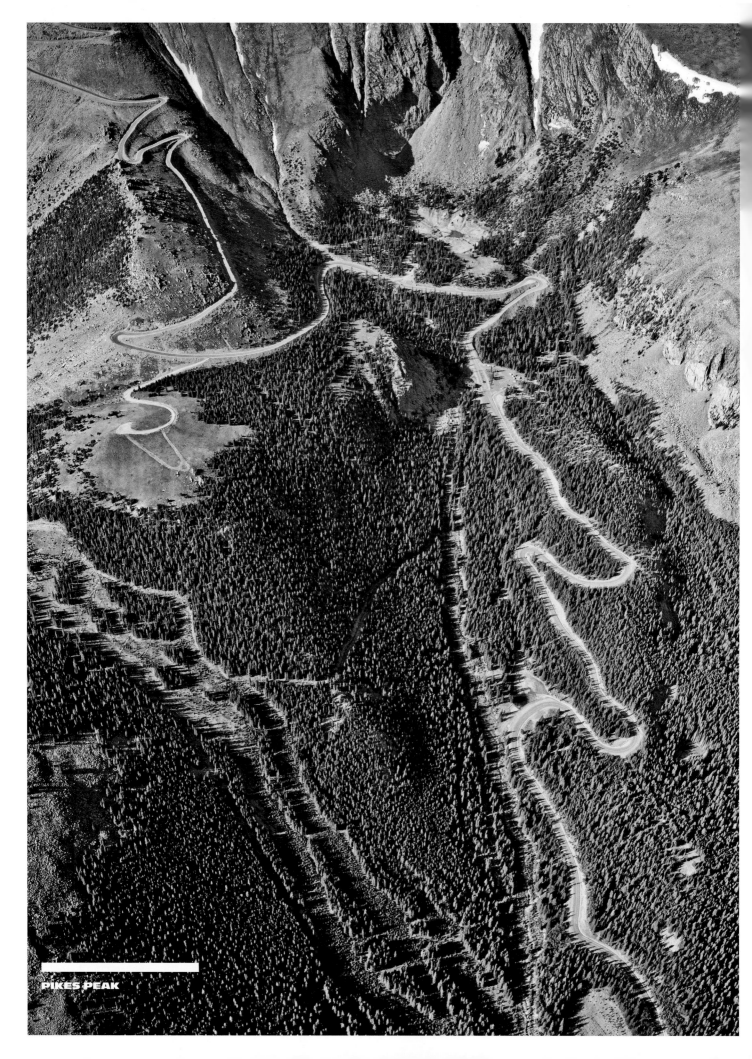

PIKES PEAK

PIKES PEAK MONTICELLO

1.650 KM • 2 TAGE // 1.025 MILES • 2 DAYS

Tiefrote Sonne über glühenden Felsen. Eine Eidechse steckt ihren Kopf aus einem Spalt zwischen den Steinen und versucht mit Zeitlupen-Bewegungen ins Freie zu kriechen, um etwas Wärme einzufangen. Oben am Gipfel des Pikes Peak zerfasern Wolken in einer Aura aus Morgenlicht, hier unten sammelt sich immer noch die Dunkelheit der Nacht wie in Schattentümpeln.

—

A crimson sun over sizzling rocks. A lizard pokes its head out of a crack in the stones and crawls in slow-mo into the open to catch some warm rays. Up at the Pikes Peak summit, wisps of clouds fly in an aura of morning light. Down here, the dark of the night still gathers like shadowy pools.

HOTEL

HOTEL JEROME
330 E MAIN ST
ASPEN, CO 81611
PHONE: 970.920.1000
WWW.AUBERGERESORTS.COM/HOTEL-
JEROME

Fünf Uhr morgens. Höchste Zeit, die Strecke hinüber zum Pikes Peak Highway zu nehmen. Heute ist Renntag. Und während sich den ganzen Sommer über die Schranke an der Tal-Mautstation erst um 7:30 Uhr für den Ansturm motorisierter Touristen öffnet, darfst du während dieses einen Wochenendes schon viel früher auf den Berg. Du musst sogar. In wenigen Stunden wird die Strecke zum Gipfel geschlossen sein, denn dann fliegen auf den 12,42 Meilen ab der Startlinie gleich hinter dem Crystal Creek Reservoir die prächtigsten Renngeräte über 1.439 Höhenmeter auf den 4.301 Meter hohen Gipfel.

Gefährlich war das Berg-Biest hinter Colorado Springs schon immer, seit dem ersten Rennen 1916, damals auf noch vollkommen unbefestigter Straße. So schnell wie in den letzten Jahren aber noch nie: Seit 2012 die Strecke mit ihren 156 Kurven komplett asphaltiert wurde, gehen die gefahrenen Zeiten nach unten. Zuerst unter 10 Minuten – mittlerweile schaffen die Schnellsten den Berg in unter 8 Minuten. Unfassbar schnell ist das. Und weil in der dünnen Höhenluft auf den letzten Meilen selbst bei hocheffizienten Verbrennungsmotoren die Leis-

It's five o'clock in the morning; high time to head off to the Pikes Peak Highway. Today is race day, and while for the entire summer the barrier at the valley toll station only opens at 7.30am for the invasion of tourists in their cars, on this particular weekend, people are permitted on the mountain much earlier. In fact, it's essential, because in a few hours the route to the summit will be closed. Then, the most magnificent racing machines will catapult off the starting line just after the Crystal Creek Reservoir and fly over the 12.42-mile route, gaining 1,439 meters of elevation to finish in the clouds at an altitude of 4,301 meters.

The mountain beast behind Colorado Springs has earned itself a dangerous reputation since the inaugural race in 1916, then still on an unpaved road. But it has never been faster than in recent years: In 2012, the route with its 156 turns was completely sealed. Driving times have plummeted, initially breaking the ten-minute barrier – today, the fastest can chew up the mountain in less than eight minutes. That's mind-bogglingly fast. And because the performance of even highly-efficient combustion engines flags in the rarefied air of the

tung kollabiert, haben Insider an „America's Mountain" längst die Ära der Elektro-Renner ausgerufen. Die drücken mit brachialem Drehmoment aus den Spitzkehren und das ohne Atemnot bis zur Ziellinie. Dafür schnüffeln mittlerweile die Fahrer im Helm an Sauerstoffflaschen, denn wer will schon beim kompromisslosen Angasen auf steilen Rampen in felsigem Gelände auch nur für einen Augenblick wegnicken? Der Berg, die Strecke, das Rennen – hier wird man noch einiges an Drama und Glorie erleben. Bevor aber der wilde Ritt losgeht, herrscht im Morgengrauen eine fast feierliche Stimmung: Teams und Zuschauer rollen die Zufahrtsstraße hinauf, zum Fahrerlager oder weiter an die Parkplätze und Campgrounds entlang der Rennstrecke. Einmal oben kommst du übrigens nicht so leicht wieder herunter, man richtet es sich also für ein Vollgasfest gemütlich ein. Hängematte zwischen Bäume gespannt, Grill aufgestellt, Bier im Kühler. Und bestenfalls ausgerüstet für alle Wetterlagen zwischen Sturm und Blitzeis und brütender Hitze. Der Pikes Peak hat es in sich. Wenn dann die ersten Helden den Berg heraufbügeln, angekündigt vom Donnern des TV-Helikopters, hast du einen der exklusivsten Plätze des Planeten. Hier oben an Glen Cove oder hinter Devil's Playground fahren die schnellsten Typen der Welt nur noch für dich. Gegen die Uhr. Für einen Platz in den Geschichtsbüchern.

Wer übrigens an einem anderen Tag des Jahres am Berg ankommt, erlebt eine gänzlich andere Atmosphäre. Bei schönem Wetter rollen Hunderte von Touristen im Bummeltempo die Mautstraße hinauf, lassen die Kameras rollen und nehmen dem Pikes Peak jeden abenteuerlichen Reiz. Wer es jetzt herausfordernd mag, sollte seine Wanderstiefel anziehen und den Berg besser zu Fuß attackieren. Soulful Walking. Auch das geht. Auf den letzten 1.000 Höhenmetern eben im Nebel des Höhenrauschs. Warm und taub zwischen den Ohren, nach Luft schnappend, mit rasendem Herzen. Die. Luft. Ist. So. Dünn.

Und dann sind wir sowieso wieder unterwegs. Lassen den Pikes Peak hinter uns und verschwinden nach Westen im Gebirge. Endgültig. Genießen das Gefühl unbändiger Freiheit. Eine Welt ohne erkennbare

last miles, insiders know that on "America's Mountain" the time of electric racers has arrived. They slingshot with brutish torque through the switchbacks, and whip to the finish line without the need to gasp for breath. Instead, the drivers now sniff air fed to their helmets from an oxygen tank; after all, no one wants to nod off through lack of air even for a moment on the sheer rocky drop-offs. The mountain, the road, the race – here there's drama and glory aplenty.

But at dawn, before the wild ride starts, the mood is somewhat festive: Teams and spectators trundle up the access roads, to the paddock or on to the parking lots and campgrounds along the racetrack. Once at the top, however, it's not so easy to get back down, so it's best to settle in for a full throttle party. String up the hammock, set up the barbecue, pop some beers in the cooler. Ready for all weather conditions from storm and freezing rain to sweltering heat. Pikes Peak ain't for the fainthearted. When the first mountain heroes roar up – announced by the whump of TV helicopters – you're in one of the most exclusive places on the planet. Up here at Glen Cove or behind Devil's Playground, the fastest guys in the world are performing just for you. Against the clock. For a place in the history books.

Incidentally, if you come up the mountain on any other day, the atmosphere is very different. When the weather is pleasant, hundreds of tourists roll up the toll road at a leisurely pace, cameras clicking, stripping every inch of adventure out of Pikes Peak. Those looking for a challenge should lace up their hiking boots and head out to explore the mountain on foot. Soulful walking. That works, too. Puffing up the last 1,000 meters in the haze of altitude euphoria. Warm and deaf between the ears, gasping for air, heart racing. The. Air. Is. So. Thin.

But then we're on the road again, leaving Pikes Peak behind and disappearing westwards into the mountain range. At last. Enjoying the feeling of unrestrained freedom. A world without any recognizable boundaries, full of possibility. Or is it just the exquisite expanse here between Denver and the back o' beyond that brings us to the edge of our senses? We know about driving

RESTAURANT

WHITE HOUSE TAVERN
302 EAST HOPKINS AVENUE
COLORADO 81611
PHONE: (970) 925-1007
WWW.ASPENWHITEHOUSE.COM

INDEPENDENCE PASS

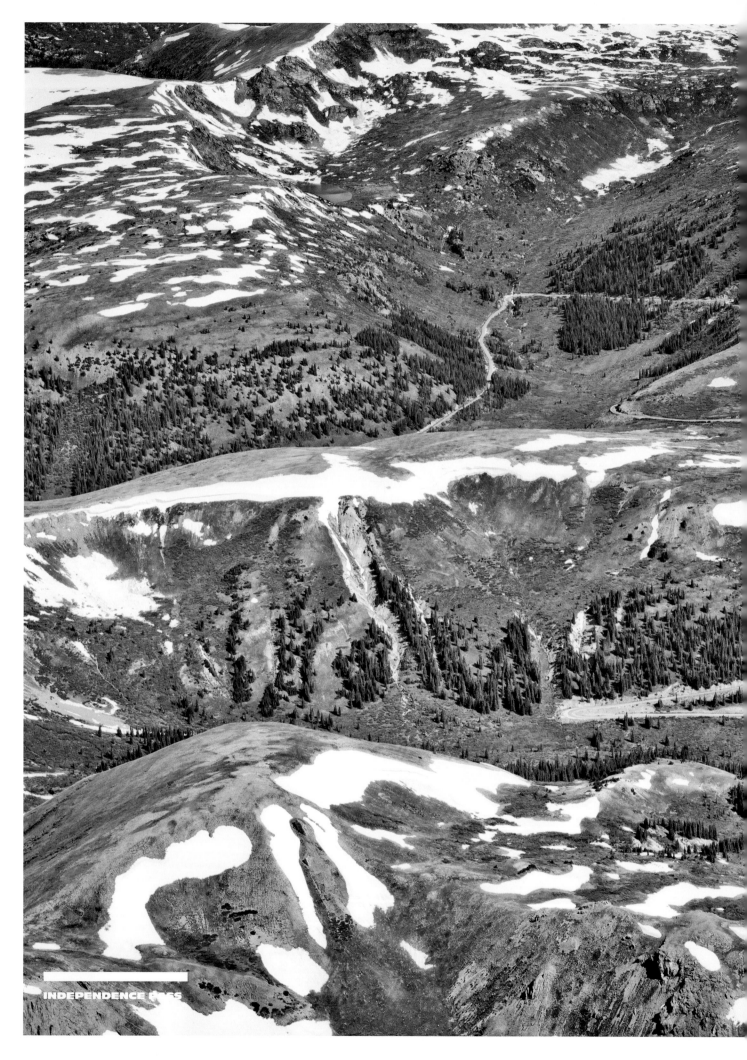

INDEPENDENCE PASS

HOTELS

STRATER HOTEL
699 MAIN AVENUE DURANGO
CO 81301
RESERVATIONS: 800.247.4431
WWW.STRATER.COM

Grenzen, voller Möglichkeiten. Oder ist es einfach nur die sagenhafte Weite, hier zwischen Denver und Nirgendwo, die uns an den Rand unseres Fassungsvermögens bringt? – Wir haben das Fahren in den Alpen gelernt, zwischen München und Venedig, und eigentlich ist das Fahren in den Rocky Mountains kaum anders. Nur eben: weiter. Viel weiter. All unsere Sensoren sind auf viel kürzere Distanzen geeicht, ab einer bestimmten Fahrdauer ohne größere menschliche Siedlungen oder Strukturen klickt in Alte-Welt-Gehirnen eine Soll-Bruchstelle und du verlierst jeglichen Bezug zu Nord-Süd-Ost-West. Zum Verständnis: Für uns CURVES-Macher gehen die Berge in Bad Tölz los und enden bei Verona. Da hast du gerade mal knappe 370 Kilometer auf der Uhr und bist bereits durch drei Staaten sowie durch mehrere Sprach- und Dialektgebiete gefahren. Mit derselben Fahrdistanz kommst du in den Rockies einmal quer über die Sawatch Range, ins Innere des Gebirges. Bereits dieses Gebiet ist elend groß – und dahinter gehen die Rocky Mountains erst richtig los. Du bist in einer Gegend gelandet, die so weit und herb ist, dass allein die Namen der Berggipfel alles erzählen. Man muss ja schon Berge im Überfluss haben, um sie Mount Harvard oder Mount Princeton zu nennen (die gebildete Variante sozusagen), Wildcat Mountain oder Sheep Mountain (noch Fragen?), Electric Mountain, Cement Mountain oder Italian Mountain. Und das sind wohlgemerkt alles nicht nur irgendwelche 10-Meter-Hügel hinter der Kirche eines Dorfs im platten Norden Deutschlands, sondern amtliche Drei- bis Über-Viertausender. Richtige Berge also. Jeder einzelne so hoch, herb und hart, dass eine Besteigung zu Fuß alle deine Reserven brauchen würde. Dazwischen erstreckt sich ein Land, das voller Wild und Natur und Einsamkeit ist. Voller Schönheit, die einen den Verstand verlieren lässt.

Diese Ecke der Welt ist durchdrungen von Legenden, der trotzige Geist der Trapper und Pioniere ist immer noch ins Land gewoben. Wer tiefer sehen kann, stößt mit den Sagen der Ureinwohner, der Arapaho und Ute, Anasazi und Comanche, auf eine beseelte Welt der Geister und Naturkräfte. Zugegeben: Wenn du hier draußen ein paar Stunden lang unterwegs bist, scheint dir die

in the Alps, we learned it between Munich and Venice, and driving here in the Rocky Mountains is not that different. Except, we go on... and on. All our sensors are calibrated towards much shorter distances, so after driving such long stretches without any major signs of human presence, the fuses in our old-world brains flip. We lose all orientation to North-South-East-West.

Just to explain: For us CURVES makers, the mountains begin in Bad Tölz and end near Verona after about 370 kilometers, and we've already driven through three countries with different languages, dialects and cultures. That same distance in the Rockies only just gets you over the Sawatch Range and into the heart of the mountains. This region is so indescribably big – and once you're through this, the real Rocky Mountains are just starting. You've arrived in a terrain that is so expansive and harsh that the names of the mountain tops alone tell the story: You'd have to have an excessive amount of mountains to allocate them names like Mount Harvard and Mount Princeton (the educated variety, so to speak), Wildcat Mountain and Sheep Mountain (any questions?), Electric Mountain, Cement Mountain and Italian Mountain. And these are not just 10-meter-high hillocks behind the church on the flat lowlands of a northern German village. These are 3,000 to over 4,000-meter-high giants. Real mountains. Each one so high, harsh and hard that to climb it on foot would take every last reserve. Between them, the land is full of wildlife, nature and solitude. Its heart-stirring beauty takes your breath away.

This corner of the world is steeped in legends; the defiant spirit of the trappers and pioneers is still woven into the land and, for those who delve deeper into the legends of the Native Americans, the Arapaho and Ute, Anasazi and Comanche, will find an inspired world of spirits and natural forces. If you spend a few hours out here, the myths surrounding Coyote and Raven don't seem too far-fetched. The land begins to swallow you, and even automotive machinery is not fast enough to shield the human mind from the powerful rush of impressions. The monotony of endless valley floors carpeted

SPEED
LIMIT
25

Zugegeben: Wenn du hier draußen ein paar Stunden lang unterwegs bist, scheint dir die Vorstellung von Bruder Kojote und Adler nicht allzu abwegig. Das Land beginnt, dich zu absorbieren, selbst die Maschine Automobil ist nicht schnell genug, um den menschlichen Geist aus den anstürmenden Eindrücken herauszulösen.

If you spend a few hours out here, the myths surrounding Coyote and Raven don't seem too far-fetched. The land begins to swallow you, and even automotive machinery is not fast enough to shield the human mind from the powerful rush of impressions.

HELI
GATEWAY CANYONS AIR TOURS
43200 CO-141, GATEWAY,
CO 81522
PHONE: +1 970-931-2740
WWW.GATEWAYCANYONSAIRTOURS.COM

MUSEUM
GATEWAY CANYONS
AUTOMOBILE MUSEUM
43224 HIGHWAY 141
GATEWAY, COLORADO 81522
PHONE: 970.931.2895
WWW.GATEWAYAUTOMUSEUM.COM

Vorstellung von Bruder Kojote und Adler nicht allzu abwegig. Das Land beginnt, dich zu absorbieren, selbst die Maschine Automobil ist nicht schnell genug, um den menschlichen Geist aus den anstürmenden Eindrücken herauszulösen. Die Monotonie endloser Talböden aus trockenem Gras wird vom plötzlichen Eintauchen in die Dramatik einer wilden Klamm abgelöst, das stetige Emporwinden der Straße bis dicht an die sommerlichen Schneefelder unter einem neonblauen Himmel weicht einen Moment später der zuckersüßen Lieblichkeit eines Tals voll quietschgelber Blümchen – das alles macht still und sprachlos. Du bist ganz klein unter einem endlosen Himmel und zwischen Bergen, die keine Notiz von dir nehmen. So schaffen wir es bis Granite am State Highway 24, gleiten dann hinüber auf die 82, vorbei an den Twin Lakes und mit Hochgefühl über den Independence Pass. Kernig im Rockabilly-Groove schmettern wir die Serpentinen hinauf. Zu diesem Zeitpunkt ahnen wir noch nicht, wie weit uns diese Etappe führen wird. Wie hypnotisch und stoisch diese magischen Meilen noch sein werden. Für die rund 250 Kilometer aus Colorado Springs am Fuß des Pikes Peak haben wir gute vier Stunden gebraucht, die wie im Flug vergangen sind. Aspen, Colorado, liegt in tiefem Sommerschlaf, Carbondale

with dry grass is broken by a sudden plunge into the drama of a wild gorge, the steady rise of the road almost reaching summer snowfields under a neon blue sky, and a moment later the sickly sweetness of a valley full of bright yellow flowers – it leaves you quiet and speechless. You are so very small under an endless sky and between mountains that take no notice of you. In this condition, we reach Granite on State Highway 24, glide over to 82, sail past Twin Lakes and, with exhilaration, over Independence Pass. Deep in rockabilly groove we blare up the serpentines, still unaware at this point of just how far this leg will take us. How hypnotic and steady these magical miles will be. The 250 kilometers from Colorado Springs at the foot of Pikes Peak took us four hours, which went by in a flash. Aspen/Colorado lies in a deep summer slumber, idyllic Carbondale at the foot of Mount Sopris in bright sunshine. The road and the driving is in our blood, we stop only to refuel and, at Hotchkiss, we take Highway 92 to the south. Past Crawford, chewing up the miles through a land full of rambling ridges towards the Gunnison River. And there, at last, the curtain goes up on a natural drama that has no equal: a river carved deep into the countryside, epic chains of hills that stretch into the wild blue yonder, and

COLORADO STATE
HIGHWAY 141

COLORADO STATE
HIGHWAY 141

ganz idyllisch am Fuß des Mount Sopris in strahlendem Sonnenschein. Die Straße und das Fahren ist uns ins Blut gegangen, nur für Tankstopps sind wir vom Lenkrad zu kriegen und deshalb nehmen wir in Hotchkiss die Abzweigung des Highway 92 nach Süden. Passieren Crawford und strömen durch ein Land voller weitläufiger Hügelketten in Richtung des Gunnison River.

Und dort geht nun endgültig der Vorhang auf zu einem Naturdrama, das seinesgleichen sucht: tief ins Land gefressener Flußlauf, epische Hügelketten, die sich bis in ein fernes Blau ziehen, und darüber eine Straße, die sich in Aussichtslage und wohliger Kurvenekstase dahinwindet. Das muss man erst einmal verkraften. Immer weiter entlang des Gunnison River, vorbei an Lake City, während im Westen der Hakenzahn des Uncompahgre Peak eine bizarre Silhouette wirft. Quer durch den Rio Grande National Forest und bei South Fork und Alpine endlich wieder in Richtung Westen. 160 Kilometer sind an diesem Nachmittag noch zu schaffen, dann rollen wir in Durango aus. Mit einem Kopf voll explodierender Eindrücke verkriechen wir uns in einen oldschool Saloon, sitzen in angenehmer Versteinerung und nehmen das Honky-Tonk-Piano erst langsam wahr. Weil plötzlich doch der linke große Zeh zu wippen beginnt und der Rhythmus durch den Körper strömt, sich in einem breiten Grinsen manifestiert. Was für ein Leben. Und Sally in ihrem schwingenden Kleid und mit dem adrett ins Haar gepinnten Hütchen will tanzen. Genau wie deine Beine.

Am nächsten Tag spürst du über 700 Kilometer lang, dass du angekommen bist, in diesem weiten, fremden Land: Honky-Tonk-Sally zwinkert dir zu, der Sportwagen hämmert vehement durch den San Juan National Forest nach Norden, in einem weiten Bogen über Montrose bis kurz vor Grand Junction, dann scharf links weg in Richtung Gateway. Jetzt hast du die Rockies endgültig hinter dir. Das Land wird rot und trocken, Felsenplateaus türmen sich entlang des Dolores River auf dem Weg nach Süden, die Straße schlängelt sich schwitzend dahin. Bis Naturita, dann über Slick Rock bis zur Grenze nach Utah. Ausrollen in Monticello. Canyonland. Aber das ist eine andere Geschichte.

Und dort geht nun endgültig der Vorhang auf zu einem Naturdrama, das seinesgleichen sucht: tief ins Land gefressener Flußlauf, epische Hügelketten, die sich bis in ein fernes Blau ziehen, und darüber eine Straße, die sich in Aussichtslage und wohliger Kurvenekstase dahinwindet. Das muss man erst einmal verkraften.

And there, at last, the curtain goes up on a natural drama that has no equal: a river carved deep into the countryside, epic chains of hills that stretch into the wild blue yonder, and a stunningly panoramic road that meanders into blissful ecstasy. It's a lot to take in.

a stunningly panoramic road that meanders into blissful ecstasy. It's a lot to take in. Tracing the Gunnison River, past Lake City, while the jagged-toothed Uncompahgre Peak shows off its bizarre silhouette in the west. Onwards through the Rio Grande National Forest to veer west again at South Fork and Alpine. After another 160 kilometers in the afternoon we pull up in Durango. Our heads exploding with impressions, we swagger into an old-school saloon, sit in pleasant stupefaction and only then notice the honky-tonk piano. Suddenly the left big toe begins to waggle, a rhythm radiates through the body, and a broad grin stretches over the face. What a life. Sally – with her wide skirt twirling and her little hat fastened prettily on her hair – wants to dance. Just like your legs.

During the 700 kilometers of the next day, you finally feel as if you've arrived in this vast, foreign land. Honky Tonk Sally winks at you, the sports car pushes vehemently on through the San Juan National Forest to the north, in a wide arc over Montrose until just before Grand Junction, then a sharp left towards Gateway. You've finally made it over the Rockies. The land turns red and arid, orange sandstone cliffs line the Dolores River. The sweltering road snakes its way south to Naturita, then Slick Rock and on to the border of Utah. We stop in Monticello. Canyonlands. But that's another story.

RESTAURANT

SWINGIN' STEAKS
100 N MAIN MEXICAN HAT
UT 84531

....

HOTEL

MEXICAN HAT LODGE
100 N MAIN MEXICAN HAT
UT 84531
WWW.MEXICANHATLODGE.COM

....

PIKES PEAK MONTICELLO

Man könnte die knapp 700 Kilometer lange Strecke von Denver, Colorado, bis zur Kleinstadt Monticello direkt hinter der Grenze zwischen Colorado und dem angrenzenden Bundesstaat Utah über die Interstate 70 in guten sechseinhalb Stunden abhaken, hätte dann ebenfalls den Hauptkamm der Rocky Mountains zur Gänze gequert und ein enormes Stück des Wegs von Denver bis an die Westküste geschafft. Aber überhaupt nicht verstanden, wie hirnzermeißelnd groß die Rocky Mountains sind. Nicht nur Ost-West, sondern auch Nord-Süd. Wie unfassbar vielfältig die Landschaften. Deshalb kreuzen wir in großen Schleifen über das Gebirge: über den Norden bei Aspen nach Carbondale, dann Hotchkiss und Lake City bis beinahe wieder in den Osten des Gebirges bei South Fork, in weitem Bogen bis Durango und erneut nach Norden. Bei Grand Junction machen wir uns auf den Weg nach Südwesten. Und jetzt endlich kennen wir die Rocky Mountains wirklich.

—

It's possible to cover the 700 or so kilometers from Denver/Colorado to the town of Monticello, just over the border between Colorado and the neighboring state of Utah via the Interstate 70, in a good six and a half hours, traversing the main ridge of the Rocky Mountains and a huge section of the route from Denver to the west coast. But in doing this, you don't quite grasp the sheer magnitude of the Rocky Mountains – not only from east to west but also north to south – and the unbelievable diversity of the landscapes. For this reason, we cross the mountains in giant loops: via the north near Aspen to Carbondale, then Hotchkiss and Lake City almost to the east of the mountains at South Fork, then a wide sweep to Durango and back to the north. At Grand Junction we head southwest. And only after this do we feel we really know the Rocky Mountains.

1.650 KM • 2 TAGE // 1.025 MILES • 2 DAYS

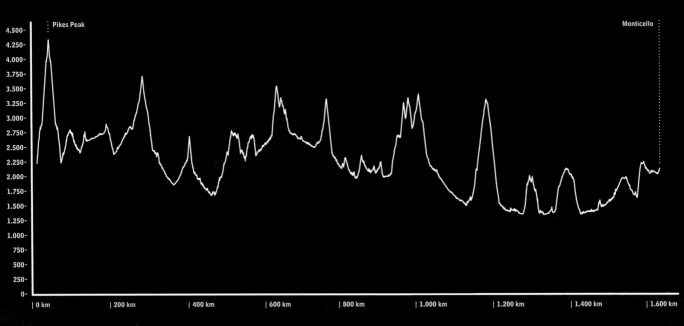

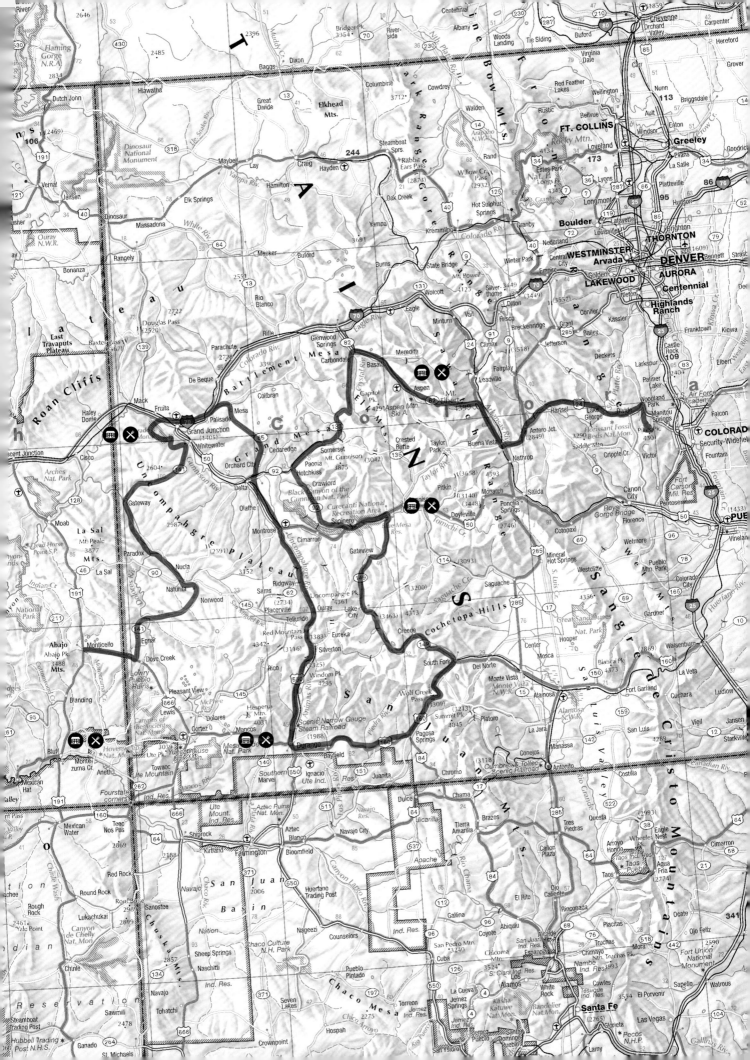

MONTICELLO MODENA

1.050 KM • 2 TAGE // 652 MILES • 2 DAYS

Es ist früh am Morgen. Kleine, braune Vögel hüpfen über den groben Kies zwischen dornentragenden Bäumen wie seltsame Außerirdische auf einem Wüstenplaneten. Sie schauen zu dir herüber, misstrauisch nickend, mit ruckartigen Bewegungen, die irgendwie bösartig wirken, wie ein Science-Fiction-Squaredance aus einer anderen Galaxie.

—

It's early morning. Like strange aliens on a desert planet, small, brown birds hop over coarse gravel between thorny trees. They peer at you, nodding suspiciously, their jerky movements somehow sinister, like a science fiction square dance from another galaxy.

MONUMENT VALLEY

Man kann diesen eigentümlichen süßen Mini-Chewbaccas eine ganze Weile zusehen, ohne sich zu langweilen. Zumindest im Utah-Modus. Der ist langsam und schräg und erstrebenswert. Rausch ohne Substanz. Einfach nur da sein und denken, was das nur für eine ungeheuerlich wilde, aufs Grobe reduzierte Welt ist. Voll herzzerreißender Schönheit. Voll kleiner Sensationen. Manchmal auch voll subtiler Komik. Bestimmt überlegen die kleinen irren Viecher gerade, wie sie dich überwältigen und in ihre Höhle schleppen können, um Alien-Experimente mit dir anzustellen.

Aber vielleicht sind es ja doch einfach nur pummelige Vögelchen, die es hier gibt, aber eben nicht da, wo du herkommst? – Ein schöner Gedanke, und so glasklar nüchtern Anti-Verschwörungstheorie, dass er leider nicht lange vorhält. Durch den rotbraunen Sand marschieren jetzt schwarze Insekten, glasig glänzend, mit Darth-Vader-Kopfmasken. Auch die sind irgendwie ... und jetzt ist Schluss.

Grinsend und kopfschüttelnd über unsere eigene Wunderlichkeit lösen wir uns vom Ausguck in den Hotelgarten. Frühstücken gehen. Cowboy-Style. Einen großen Teller voller Eier, Würstchen, Paprika, Zwiebeln und natürlich Chilisauce. Dazu eine mächtige Tasse Perkolator-Kaffee, bei dem es immer Glücksache ist, ob du den faden Anfang erwischst, die erträgliche Mitte oder den Herzinfarkt-induzierenden Schluss. Rabenschwarzer, intravenöser Koffein-Tod. Bittere Galle. In den USA nennen sie so etwas tatsächlich Kaffee. Italiener und Araber würden Auge in Auge mit diesem metallisch schmeckenden, Altöl-artigen Etwas den sofortigen Freitod wählen. Hier in Monticello, Utah, hältst du der Bedienung aber ungerührt den Becher hin und nimmst einen Refill. Keine Ahnung weshalb. Eine geistige Umnachtung namens Cowboy-Gefühl vielleicht? – Irgendwie ertappst du dich ja sogar, wie du Eier und Bohnen in großen Mengen schaufelst, mit Löffel statt Gabel und dem Daumen oben am Löffelstiel. Leicht schmatzend und dazwischen eben immer wieder einen Schluck Altöl schlürfend. Du hast das in einem Film aus den Siebzigern gesehen, in dem Männer Schnauzbärte trugen, verschwitzte

It's easy to watch these oddly sweet little "Chewbaccas" for quite some time without getting bored. At least if you're in Utah mode. This state is slow and quirky and worthwhile. Intoxication without substance. Simply just being there and thinking what an outrageously wild world this is, reduced to the essential things. Full of heart-wrenching beauty. Full of small wonders. And sometimes full of subtle comedy. Surely these crazy little critters are thinking about how they will overpower you and drag you into their caves to conduct alien experiments on you.

But perhaps they are simply chubby little birds that are from here but not from where you live? A nice thought: crystal clear and so very anti-conspiracy theory. Unfortunately it doesn't last for long. Marching through the reddish-brown sand come black insects wearing shiny Darth Vader head masks. They too seem somehow... okay, that's enough now.

Grinning and shaking our heads at our own whimsicality, we pry ourselves away from our garden reverie. Time for breakfast. Cowboy style. A huge plate piled with eggs, sausages, bell peppers, onions and, of course, lashings of chili sauce. Plus a strong cup of percolated coffee – it's always a matter of luck whether you get the weak beginning, the bearable middle, or the heart-attack-inducing dregs. Jet black, death by intravenous caffeine. Bitter bile. They actually call this coffee in America. Confronted with this metallic, rancid-oil-tasting stuff, Italians and Arabs would promptly commit suicide. Here in Monticello/Utah, you philosophically hold up your cup for the waitress to refill. No idea why. Perhaps a mental blackout called cowboy feeling?

Somehow, you even catch yourself shoveling eggs and beans into your mouth with a spoon instead of a fork, with your thumb sticking straight up from the handle. With a slight lip-smack and a slurp of rancid oil. You saw this once in a 1970s film with walrus-moustached men wearing sweat-stained plaid shirts and tight trousers. By this point, you would've noticed that something was wrong, because no one can

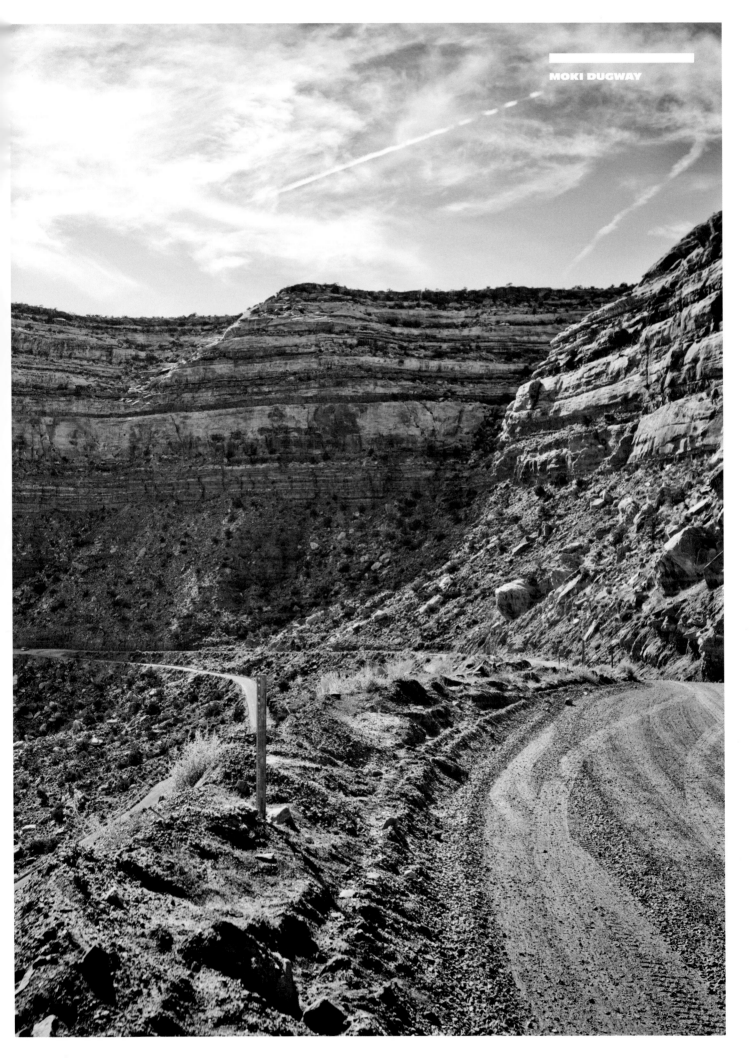

Karohemden und enge Hosen. Spätestens da hätte man merken können, dass etwas ganz und gar nicht stimmt, denn kein Mensch kann tagelang in engen Hosen auf einem Pferd durch den Wilden Westen reiten. Echte Cowboys hatten weite Hosen. Aber das ist jetzt ja auch nur wieder irgendeine nutzlose Feststellung deines auf Hochtouren laufenden Gehirns.

Es zieht dich hinaus. Zuerst auf den dicken Teppich im Flur zum Hotelzimmer, mit dem in den USA jedes Motel oder Hotel standardmäßig ausgelegt wird. Der Teppich kommt gerüchtehalber aus einer großen Fabrik irgendwo in Atlanta, riecht immer gleich (erstaunlicherweise auch nach ein bis zwei Jahrzehnten) und es gibt ihn gefühlt in drei Abwandlungen ein und desselben Musters. Denkst du tatsächlich schon über Teppiche nach? – Nichts wie weg! Tasche schnappen, zur Rezeption und ein paar Sekunden später sitzt du am Steuer. Das Auto ist noch kühl von der Nacht. Scheint sich zu räkeln, zu strecken und erst langsam auf Betriebstemperatur zu kommen. Langsam rollen wir auf die Straße hinaus. Bleiben an der letzten Ampel vor der langen Geraden am Ortsausgang stehen. Starren in ein grau-rot-beiges Nichts, durch das sich sanft flimmernd ein grauer Asphaltstreifen zieht und auf dem ein gelber Mittelstrich dahinschlingert. Gerade ist eben doch relativ. Gibt es vielleicht gar nicht auf diesem Planeten, der immer irgendwie die Biege macht. Heute könnte ein guter Tag sein, um dieser Sache auf den Grund zu gehen. Und deshalb: Los.

Irgendwann, viel später, stellst du fest, dass „Geradeausfahren" eigentlich nur ein Aggregatzustand des Kurvenfahrens ist. Andere Temperatur, anderer Siedepunkt. In deinem Kopf rollt die Straße unaufhörlich ab und das geht so weiter, selbst wenn du abends ins Bett fällst. Man muss sich allerdings ganz bestimmt keine Sorgen machen, dass da mentalgesundheitlich etwas aus der Spur gerät, denn menschliche Gehirne denken bevorzugt geradeaus. Das ist die Komfortzone. Stetige Wiederholung. Sicherheit. Kalkulierbares Risiko, minimales Überraschungspotenzial. Das bisschen Einöde verkraftest du locker. Kurven sind dagegen so etwas wie der Säbelzahntiger

ride through the Wild West for days wearing such tight trousers. Real cowboys had wide britches. But that's just another useless observation of a brain running at full revs.

It's time to leave. First over the thick carpet in the hallway – a standard floor covering in every motel and hotel in the USA. The carpet apparently comes from a big factory somewhere in Atlanta, and it always smells the same (astoundingly even after a decade or two) and it seems as if there are three variations of the same pattern. Are you really thinking about carpets? Let's get out of here! Grab your bag, head to reception, and a few seconds later you're at the wheel. The car is still cool from the night. It seems to twitch, stretch and only slowly warms up. We roll out onto the road. Stopping at the last traffic light before the long straight out of town. Staring into a gray-red-beige nothingness, through which a gray asphalt stripe gently flickers and a yellow median line sways. Straight ahead is just relative. Is everything on this planet somehow bent? Today might be a good day to get to the bottom of this matter. And so, off we go.

At some point, much later, you realize that "driving straight ahead" is actually only an aggregate state of cornering. Different temperature, different boiling point. The road keeps rolling unrelentingly in your head and continues like this even after you fall asleep at night. Still, you don't have to worry about your mental health, because human brains are programmed to think straight. That's called the comfort zone. Constant repetition, security, calculable risk. Minimal potential for surprise. You can easily cope with a little boredom. Curves, on the other hand, are something like the saber-toothed tiger at the entrance of your sleeping cave: you hadn't expected this, damn it. Immediate adrenaline rush and action... yet still, despite our adoration of the twisty passages, we've recently started a little love affair with driving straight on. Maybe you should try it too. After Monticello, we continue on Highway 191 to the south towards Blanding and on to Bluff. The Earth's crust here seems to have formed a million-year-old scab, slow-

HOTEL & RESTAURANT

BROKEN SPUR INN & STEAKHOUSE
955 EAST SR 24
TORREY, UT 84775
WWW.BROKENSPURINN.COM

RESTAURANT

CAFE DIABLO
599 WEST MAIN STREET
TORREY, UT, 84775
PHONE: 435-425-3070
WWW.CAFEDIABLO.COM

UTAH STATE ROUTE 95

CAFE

KIVA COFFEEHOUSE
7386 HWY 12 MILE MARKER
ESCALANTE, UT 84726
WWW.KIVAKOFFEEHOUSE.COM

im Eingang der Schlafhöhle: Mit dem hättest du jetzt irgendwie nicht gerechnet, verdammt nochmal. Sofortige Adrenalinausschüttung und Action ... – Und trotzdem. Trotz dieses Lobpreises der Kurvenstrecken haben wir neuerdings eine kleine Liebesaffäre mit dem Geradeausfahren am Laufen. Vielleicht versuchen Sie es ja auch mal: Hinter Monticello den Highway 191 nach Süden in Richtung Blanding fahren, bis nach Bluff. Die Erdkruste scheint hier einen Millionen Jahre alten Schorf gebildet zu haben. Langsam, Stück für Stück, fährt man von einer Schicht in die nächste, bis die Straße vor Bluff in einen Canyon schneidet, um dann auf dem Grund eines Urzeit-Meeres in Sichtweite des San Juan River dahinzu-

ly, piece by piece; we drive from one layer to the next, until the road before Bluff cuts into a canyon, and then flies along the bottom of a prehistoric ocean with the San Juan River in sight. Only at Mexican Hat does the broiling tarmac stripes venture close to the river. Here, the San Juan meets a rock barrier, forcing it through the Gooseneck State Park in countless loops.

From here we're supposed to head north over Hanksville and the Grand Staircase-Escalante National Park to Bryce and on to Cedar City, but the detour to the Arizona border and into the expanse of Monument Valley proves irresistible. Thirty-five kilometers to the south, thirty-five back. Piece

UTAH HIGHWAY 12
SCENIC BYWAY

BRYCE CANYON

fliegen. Erst bei Mexican Hat traut sich der glühende Asphaltstreifen an den Fluss heran, hier rennt der San Juan gegen eine Gesteinsbarriere an, die ihn in die unzähligen Schleifen des Gooseneck State Parks zwingt.

Eigentlich soll es ab hier nach Norden gehen, über Hanksville und den Grand Staircase-Escalante Nationalpark bis Bryce und weiter nach Cedar City, aber der Abstecher zur Grenze nach Arizona und in die Weite des Monument Valley muss einfach sein. 35 Kilometer nach Süden, 35 zurück. Fahren wir heute auf einer Pobacke, denn geradeaus, das ist unser Leben. Und der Moment, in dem wir eine halbe Stunde später das Auto unter bis zu 300 Meter hohen Tafelbergen in ziegelroter Einöde abstellen, ist jeden gefahrenen Kilometer wert. Als wären wir in einer Raumkapsel auf Rädern zum Mars geflogen. Auf einen eisenoxidroten Planeten aus versteinertem Feuer.

Auf dem Rückweg sind plötzlich wilde Mustangs auf der Straße. Mager und zerzaust kommen sie aus der Steppe, die langen Mähnen flattern im Wind. Wir stoppen den Wagen und lassen die Herde passieren. Ein rostrot gescheckter Schimmel schlendert dicht an unserem Auto vorbei, mit hängendem Kopf und aufmerksamen Augen, eine sonderbare Mischung aus absoluter Gelassenheit und hellwacher Nervosität. Selbst als die Tiere nur noch kleine Punkte vor den Felsgiganten des Tals sind, sitzen wir noch ruhig im Auto und freuen uns über diese Begegnung. Dann ziehen auch wir weiter. Zurück nach Mexican Hat, vorbei an den typisch breitkrempigen Felsformationen. Weiter nach Norden bis zur Brücke über den Colorado River. Der strebt hier in einem tiefen Tal voller Grün über die Oberfläche des Wüstenplaneten einem Rendezvous mit dem San Juan River entgegen. In den Hügeln des Capitol Reefs wird es noch einmal kurvig. Das Hin- und Herschwingen der Straße zwischen aufgefalteten Gesteinsschichten, bröckelnden Rampen und hohen Felsdomen ist nach den vielen Meilen auf schnurgeraden Straßen so überraschend, dass wir tatsächlich eine Weile benötigen, um auf einen neuen Fahr-Rhythmus umzustellen. Gerade rechtzeitig für den turbulenten Highway 12 über Boulder

Eigentlich soll es ab hier nach Norden gehen, über Hanksville und den Grand Staircase-Escalante Nationalpark bis Bryce und weiter nach Cedar City, aber der Abstecher zur Grenze nach Arizona und in die Weite des Monument Valley muss einfach sein.

From here we're supposed to head north over Hanksville and the Grand Staircase-Escalante National Park to Bryce and on to Cedar City, but the detour to the Arizona border and into the expanse of Monument Valley proves irresistible.

of cake, because straight ahead is our life. And when we stop the car half an hour later under 300-meter-high flat-top mountains set in the brick-red desert, it was worth every extra kilometer. As if we've flown to Mars in a space capsule on wheels to an iron-oxide-red planet made of petrified fire.

On the way back, wild Mustangs suddenly appear on the road. Skinny and unkempt, they emerge from the prairie, their long manes fluttering in the wind. We stop the car and let the herd pass. A rust-red brindle horse wanders close to our car, head drooping, eyes watchful, a strange combination of complete serenity and alert skittishness. Even when the animals are just specks against the rock giants of the valley, we sit quietly in the car, contemplating what we've just experienced. We, too, giddy-up. Back to Mexican Hat, past the distinctive, wide-brimmed rock formations. Further on to the north, to the bridge over the Colorado River, which flows through a deep, verdant valley over a desert planet on its way to a rendezvous with the San Juan River.

In the hills of Capitol Reef the route gets twisty again. The writhing of the road between folded stone strata, crumbling slopes and high rock domes comes as such a surprise after the many miles of dead-straight roads; it actually takes us a while

HOTEL & RESTAURANT

RUBYS INN
26 SOUTH MAIN STREET
BRYCE CANYON CITY
UTAH 84764
WWW.RUBYSINN.COM

ZION NATIONAL PARK

SNOW CANYON
STATE PARK

und Escalante nach Süden. Als wir nach beinahe drei Stunden Fahrt den Bryce Canyon erreichen, steht die Sonne tief und schickt ihre Strahlen blitzend unter Wolkenfetzen hindurch. Den Fußmarsch im Canyon lassen wir jetzt aus: Für die letzten Meilen rüber nach Modena durch den Zion National Park werden wir jede Minute Tageslicht brauchen und durch mindestens ebenso spektakuläres Land fahren.

Abendsonne fängt sich in den Baumkronen der uns zuerst begleitenden Pinienwälder, immer wieder brechen aus dichter Vegetation markante Felsformationen, dann wird das Land hinter Mount Carmel Junction trockener und weiter. Tanzt durch den Zion National Park. Grooving like a Lion in Zion. Das träge Philosophieren der langen Etappen auf schnurgeraden Linien ist nun nur noch eine wunderliche Erinnerung. Aber nicht für lang, denn es folgt wieder ein Erdgeschichtslehrgang in Gesteinsform. Sehen, staunen, leuchten. Wir sind alle nur ein Funke. Hinter St. George geht es auf dem Highway 18 nach Norden, bei Beryl Junction nach Osten. Direkt vor uns endet Utah. Blauschwarze Nacht frisst eine verglühende Sonne. Nevada voraus. Das große Nichts.

to change to a new driving rhythm. Just in time for the turbulent Highway 12 via Boulder and Escalante to the south. When we reach Bryce Canyon after almost three hours of driving, the sun sits low and sends its sparkling rays under the wispy clouds. We decide against a walk in the canyon: for the last miles to Modena through the Zion National Park, we will need every minute of daylight and the countryside on this stretch will be just as spectacular.

The evening sun catches in the treetops of the pine forest that have just appeared, with rock formations peaking time and again out above the dense vegetation, before the country after Mount Carmel Junction becomes drier and wider. We dance through the Zion National Park. Grooving like a lion in Zion. The lazy philosophizing of the long leg on a dead straight line is now just a hazy and wonderful memory. But not for long, because once again a geological history class in rock form presents itself. See, marvel, be. We're all just sparks. After St. George we take Highway 18 to the north, turning east at Beryl Junction. Utah ends right here. Blue-black night eats the scorching sun. Ahead is Nevada. The big emptiness.

SNOW CANYON
STATE PARK

MONTICELLO MODENA

Nach den Etappen der Rocky Mountains von Colorado steuern wir auf der dritten Etappe in eine ganz neue Landschaft hinein: Die Canyonlands des US-Bundesstaats Utah sind schroff, magisch und einsam. Den Beginn machen die Streckenabschnitte hinunter zur ehemaligen Uran-Bergbaustadt Bluff. Dann geht es am wilden San Juan River entlang, der mit seinen tief ins Gestein gefrästen Schleifen unglaubliche Landschaften geschaffen hat. Hinter Mexican Hat muss es ein Abstecher ins Monument Valley sein: Die majestätischen Tafelberge in einsamer und endloser Weite sind Fotomotiv Nummer Eins einer Reise durch den Wilden Westen. Ähnlich derbe und trocken zieht sich das Land dem Verlauf des Colorado River entgegen, dann queren wir den Capitol Reef National Park. Bei Hanksville haben wir den nördlichsten Punkt dieser Etappe erreicht und starten nun die Durchquerung der beiden großen Nationalparks rund um das Capitol Reef und das Grand Staircase-Escalante Monument. Vorbei am Bryce Canyon und durch den Zion Nation Park schließen wir diese Fahrt durch Utah ab. Weite Strecken, aber Landschaften wie aus einem Traum.

—

After the stages through the Rocky Mountains of Colorado, we head into a whole new landscape on leg three: the Canyonlands of the US state of Utah are rugged, magical and lonely. First, the route leads down to the former uranium mining town of Bluff, then along the wild San Juan River, with its loops carved deep into the awe-inspiring landscape. After Mexican Hat, a detour into Monument Valley is a must: the majestic flat-topped butts in an isolated, endless expanse are the number one photo opportunity on a journey through the Wild West. Equally as rugged and dry, the land stretches along the Colorado River; we then cross the Capitol Reef National Park. At Hanksville we reach the northernmost point of this leg and now start to traverse the two large national parks around Capitol Reef and the Grand Staircase-Escalante Monument. Passing Bryce Canyon and through the Zion National Park, we conclude the drive through Utah. It's a long trip, but the landscapes are a dream.

1.050 KM • 2 TAGE // 652 MILES • 2 DAYS

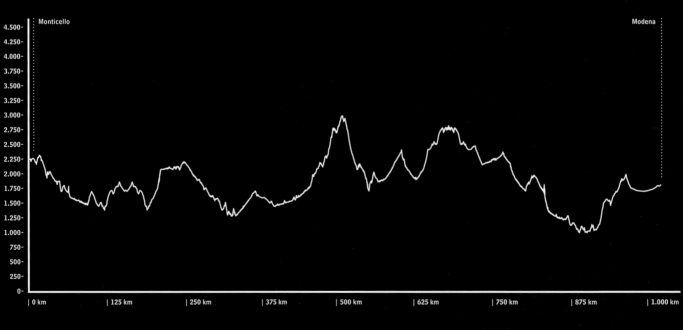

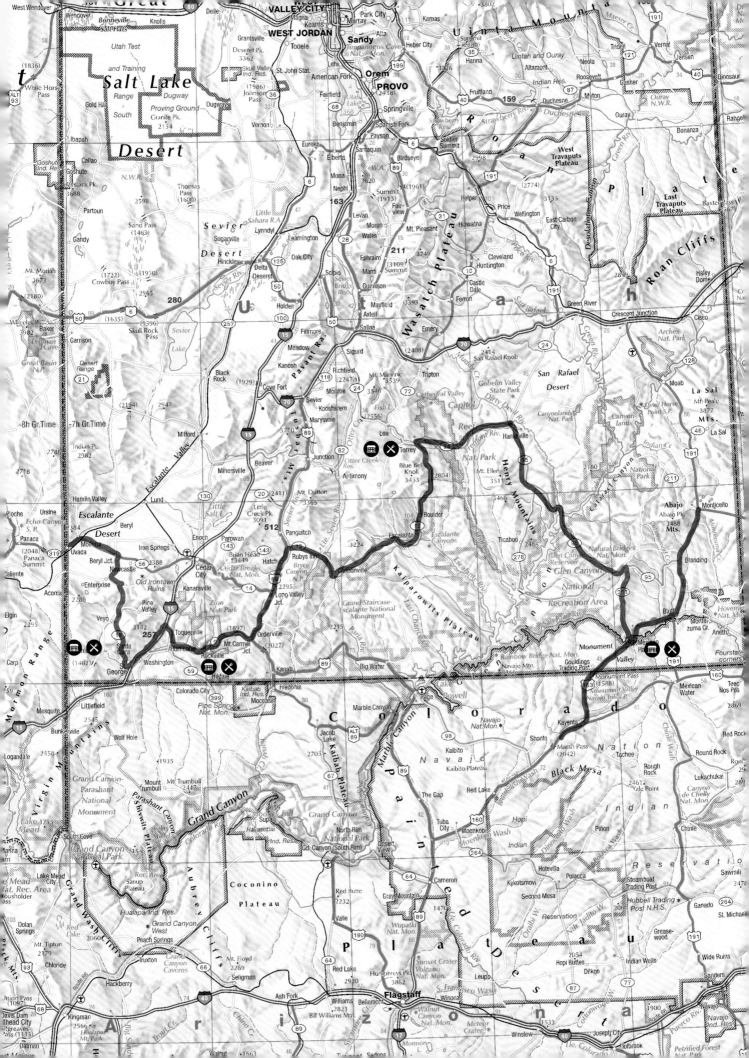

MODENA
LAKE TAHOE

800 KM • 1,5 TAGE // 498 MILES • 1,5 DAYS

„Ground Control to Major Tom …" David Bowie nörgelt das scheinbar gelangweilt dahin, in einem staubtrockenen Land zwischen gepresstem Bariton und mattem Tenor. Er scheint beim Singen gewusst zu haben, dass wir das heute hören werden, auf den knapp 140 Kilometern zwischen der östlichen Staatsgrenze von Nevada und Crystal Springs.

—

Ground Control to Major Tom… as we drive through a baked-dry land, David Bowie drones on, obviously bored, switching between a forced baritone and weary tenor. It's almost as if he knew when he sang this song that we'd listen to it today, on the 140 or so kilometers between the eastern border of Nevada and Crystal Springs.

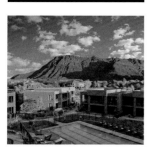

HOTEL & RESTAURANT

RED MOUNTAIN RESORT
1275 RED MOUNTAIN CIR
IVINS, UT 84738
PHONE: +1 435-673-4905
WWW.REDMOUNTAINRESORT.COM

„For here am I sitting in a tin can, far above the world", steigt der Mann auf dem Beifahrersitz ein und schaut wissend herüber, während draußen die Wüste von der stählernen, eiskalt glühenden Glasigkeit des späten Vormittags übernommen wird. „Planet Earth is blue, and there's nothing I can do", zuckst du mit den Schultern. Schön, zusammen allein zu sein. Auf einer Reise ans Ende des bekannten Universums und darüber hinaus. Gleichmäßig fliegt die automobile Raumkapsel dahin, im Inneren herrscht wieder Schweigen. Nur die Stimme von Major Tom ist noch da: „Though I'm past one hundred thousand miles I'm feeling very still and I think my spaceship knows which way to go."

Manchmal nähert man sich hier draußen Wohnmobilen, die wie stumpfsinnige Grasfresser übers Land ziehen, mit gesenkten Köpfen, mächtigem Panzer und stampfenden, röchelnden Maschinen. Sie tragen pathetische Namen in verblichenen Farben auf von UV-Strahlung spröde gekochter Kunststoffhaut – Explorer, Roadrunner oder Trailblazer – und wenn man sie dahinschuften sieht, weiß man: Sleeper, Creeper oder Obstructor wären passendere Bezeichnungen für diese muffigen Geschöpfe mit Innenleben aus einem Albtraum in dunkler Eiche. Ein paar Sekunden lang arbeiten wir uns von hinten herantreibend in den Windschatten des Wohngiganten, dann geht es ab auf die linke Spur und vorbei. – Dies sind später die Momente, über die man zurück in Europa erzählen wird, dass es überhaupt nicht schlimm ist, Hunderte von Meilen lang nicht schneller als 70 Meilen pro Stunde – 112 km/h schnell – zu fahren. Dass einem der stoische Groove auf den endlosen Geraden des Westens irgendwie ins Blut geht, geheimnisvoll entschleunigend und eine Ehrfurcht vor den Distanzen hervorrufend. Wenn du aber irgendwo auf der 94 in Richtung Crystal Springs zwischen 70-Meilen-Tempolimit und einem mit 68,3 Meilen Topspeed dahinwummernden Explore-the-West-Camper vegetierst, fällt dir auf einmal ein, dass dein Auto ja über 400 PS hat. Über 300 km/h schnell sein könnte. Und dass dieser Moment bleiernen Dahinziehens innerhalb eines Sekundenbruchteils aufgelöst werden könnte. Einfach Gas geben.

"For here am I sitting in a tin can, far above the world," the guy in the passenger seat sings along and glances over knowingly. Outside, the desert is cloaked in the steely, ice-cold glowing glassiness of the late morning. "Planet Earth is blue, and there's nothing I can do," you shrug.

It's nice being alone together. On a journey to the end of the known Universe and beyond. Smooth and sleek, the automobile space capsule flies on; inside there's silence, except for the voice of Major Tom: "Though I'm past one hundred thousand miles, I'm feeling very still and I think my spaceship knows which way to go."

Every so often, we encounter recreational vehicles out here, drifting across the land like mindless grass-eaters, heads bowed, mighty frames, and stomping, snorting engines. They have pathetic names in faded colors on plastic skin, brittle from the UV rays: Explorer, Roadrunner or Trailblazer – and when you see them lethargic and sluggish you know that Sleeper, Creeper or Obstructer would be a more fitting description for these fusty creatures with the inner workings of a nightmare made of dark oak. For a few seconds we trail in the lee of a rolling behemoth before veering on to the left lane and whipping past. These will be the moments that will be shared later with the ones back in Europe: that it's not at all annoying to cover hundreds of miles at just 70 miles per hour, or 112 km/h. That somehow the stoic groove over the endless straights of the West gets into your blood, mysteriously easing the pace, the sheer distance evoking a certain reverence. But when you're caught on the 94 heading to Crystal Springs between a 70 mph speed limit area and an Explore-the-West-Camper dawdling along at a top speed of 68.3 mph, it suddenly dawns on you that your car puts out more than 400 horsepower. It could go faster than 300 kilometers per hour. And this leaden torture could be over within a fraction of a second. You just have to put down the throttle pedal. Sense how the car gathers speed. How the sails fill out. How the vast expanse suddenly becomes manageable. For a moment you revel in the liberating idea of flying to the horizon at warp speed. This land

EXTRATERRESTRIAL
HIGHWAY

EXTRATERRESTRIAL
HIGHWAY

Spüren, wie die Maschine schneller und schneller wird. Wie sich die Segel blähen. Wie der weite Raum plötzlich beherrschbar wird. Einen Moment lang schwelgst du in der befreienden Vorstellung, dem Horizont mit Warp-Speed entgegenzufliegen. Dieses Land könnte trivial werden. Die Distanz belanglos. Und genau das ist die eigentlich schockierende Erkenntnis: Der Preis der Geschwindigkeit ist zu hoch. Nicht, weil die Highway Patrol hier draußen durchaus ein waches Auge hat, sondern weil du mit steigendem Tempo einfach abhebst. Das Land geht dir verloren, die Momente verschwimmen. Die Sterne dieser Milchstraße im beinahe menschenleeren Raum bleiben zurück. Und genau aus diesem Grund würden wir in den Momenten auf der Überholspur mit 72 Meilen auf der Uhr manchmal sogar lieber noch langsamer fahren. Vielleicht die Zeit zurückdrehen und mit dem Planwagen über die Ebene ziehen, oder auf einem Pferd. Automobile haben eine ernüchternd bürokratische Art, Entfernungen zurückzulegen. Blick auf den Kilometerzähler: 236, 237, 238 …

Was muss das für ein Gefühl sein, jetzt stattdessen von einem Pferderücken herab das Terrain zu lesen. Weichen Sand von besser zu querenden Schotterfeldern zu unterscheiden. Rinnen im Boden zu umgehen. Auf der Hut vor Schlangen oder Skorpionen zu sein. Die Hitze der Sonne zu spüren und im nächsten Moment einen kühlen Windstoß, der einen unter verschwitzter Kleidung frösteln lässt … An diesem dahingeträumten Moment angekommen, fängst du an, das Land wirklich wahrzunehmen. Der Blick schweift neben die Straße. Du siehst anders. Zwischen sandigen Becken mit enormen Abmessungen verlaufen Hügelketten auf denen sich Gestrüpp und harte Büsche oder manchmal sogar niedrige Nadelwälder ausbreiten, man nähert sich diesen Zonen der Illusion wie in Zeitlupe. Weit voraus erscheinen sie als dunkle Streifen am Horizont, ohne näherzukommen. Nur an der stetigen Entfernung vom letzten Fixpunkt im Rückspiegel ist zu erkennen, dass wir uns überhaupt bewegen. Irgendwann gerät dann alles in Schwebe, nichts entfernt sich, nichts rückt heran. Nur die Maschine summt, der Raum um uns dreht sich in Endlosschleife. Und dann, irgend-

Einen Moment lang schwelgst du in der befreienden Vorstellung, dem Horizont mit Warp-Speed entgegenzufliegen. Dieses Land könnte trivial werden. Die Distanz belanglos. Und genau das ist die eigentlich schockierende Erkenntnis: Der Preis der Geschwindigkeit ist zu hoch. Nicht, weil die Highway Patrol hier draußen durchaus ein waches Auge hat, sondern weil du mit steigendem Tempo einfach abhebst.

For a moment you revel in the liberating idea of flying to the horizon at warp speed. This land could become less overwhelming – the distance irrelevant. And this realization is rather shocking: the price of speed is too high. Not because the Highway Patrol around these parts is particularly alert, but because you simply disengage with increasing speed.

could become less overwhelming – the distance irrelevant. And this realization is rather shocking: the price of speed is too high. Not because the Highway Patrol around these parts is particularly alert, but because you simply disengage with increasing speed. You lose sight of the land, the moments blur. The stars of this Milky Way in an almost uninhabited space are left behind. And for this very reason, we would sometimes prefer to take it even slower than the 72 miles per hour in the fast lane. Perhaps turn back the clock and roll across the plains in a covered wagon or on a horse. Cars having a sobering, bureaucratic way of covering distances: just look at the odometer, 236, 237, 238...

How must it feel to read the terrain from the back of a horse? To distinguish soft sand from the more easily navigable gravel fields. To avoid ruts in the earth. Be on the lookout for snakes or scorpions. Feel the heat of the sun and the next moment a cool gust of wind that makes you shiver in your sweaty clothes. Grasping this imaginary moment, you truly perceive the country. Your eyes scan the roadside. You see differently. Between sandy basins of enormous breadth, brushwood, hardy shrubs and sometimes even stunted pine forests spread along the ridges. One

HOTEL & RESTAURANT

MIZPAH HOTEL
100 N MAIN ST, TONOPAH
NV 89049
PHONE: +1 855-337-3030
WWW.THEMIZPAHHOTEL.COM

wann, nachdem viele kostbare Minuten deines mit Glück 80 oder 90 Jahre währenden Lebens vergangen sind, ist doch eine Veränderung wahrzunehmen. Minimales Größenwachstum. Als hätte man an einem Zoom-Objektiv unmerklich ein paar Millimeter herangedreht. So geht das Minute um Minute. Immer weiter weg vom „Dahinten" und immer dichter ans „Vorn".

Auf dem Navigationssystem ist nur ein schräger Strick eingezeichnet, keine Ortschaften, keine abzweigenden Straßen, nichts. Jetzt schaust du gern auch mal auf die Tankanzeige, denn hier draußen ist eine solide Reichweite Schlüssel zu tiefer Entspannung. Zweistellige Reichweiten lösen sofortige Schweißauflage aus, denn die nächste Tankstelle ist weit entfernt. In einem anderen Sonnensystem. Ganz bestimmt möchte man aber auf dem Weg dorthin nicht liegenbleiben. Überall sonst eigentlich auch nicht – aber ganz bestimmt nicht hier. Nicht zwischen Crystal Springs, Rachel und Warm Springs. Dies ist der Extraterrestrial Highway. Wer weiß schon, was in direkter Nachbarschaft zur Area 51 wirklich passiert. Und natürlich siehst du jetzt die Anhalter neben der Straße schon von Weitem stehen. Du hast ja genügend Zeit. Ein einsames, kleines Auto, daneben zwei Wesen. Vermutlich Homo Sapiens. Wer weiß das hier draußen schon?

„Was jetzt?", rast es in deinem Kopf. „Hat das etwas mit mir zu tun?" Plötzlich ist die kontemplative Einkehr der letzten Stunden zum Teufel, alles scheint sich nur noch um diese Leute da vorn zu drehen. Stand ein paar Meilen vorher nicht dieses Warnschild, man solle wegen einer nahegelegenen Justizvollzugsanstalt keine Anhalter mitnehmen? Oder war das vorgestern? Intuitiv drehst du am Tempomat ein paar km/h zurück, du brauchst schließlich Bedenkzeit in diesem Moment beklemmender Überraschung. Und dann bist du endlich dicht genug, um alles zu sehen: keine Säbelzahntiger, keine Marsianer, niemand von Alpha Centauri oder noch weiter draußen, stattdessen zwei Ladies. Eine forsch winkend neben dem Auto, die andere schüchtern ein paar Meter entfernt. Hat wohl zu viele Thriller gesehen, in denen brave Anhalter-Mädchen draußen in der Wüste von Kanni-

approaches these zones of illusion as if in slow motion. Far ahead, they appear as dark streaks on the horizon, without coming closer. Only putting a steady distance between us and the last fixed point in the rear-view mirror can we see that we're actually moving. Somehow everything becomes suspended, nothing moves away, nothing comes closer. Just the hum of the engine, the space around us revolves in an endless loop. And then, at some point, after many precious minutes of your life have passed, a life which may span 80 or 90 years with luck, there's a change. A tiny increase in size. As if, imperceptibly, a lens has zoomed in a few millimeters. And so the minutes go by. Always further away from what's left behind and always closer to what's ahead.

The navigation system shows a diagonal line: no towns, no turnoffs, nothing. You glance at the fuel gauge, because out here a decent cruising range is paramount for deep relaxation. Two-digit ranges trigger an immediate lather of cold sweat – the next gas station is far away. In another solar system. One certainly wouldn't want to run out on the way there. Nowhere else either for that matter, but definitely not here. Not between Crystal Springs, Rachel and Warm Springs. This is the Extraterrestrial Highway. Who really knows what happens here with Area 51 close by? Suddenly, of course, you notice the hitchhikers far up ahead standing next to the road. You have plenty of time. A lonely, small car, two creatures next to it. Probably Homo sapiens. Who really knows way out here?

Thoughts whirl through your mind. What's this? Are they waiting for me? Suddenly the contemplative reverie of the last hours is shattered; everything now seems to revolve around these people up ahead. Wasn't there a warning sign a few miles back forbidding the picking up of hitchhikers in light of the nearby correctional facility? Or was that the day before yesterday? Intuitively, you slow your speed by a couple of km/h, you need time to think this disturbing surprise through. And then you're finally close enough to see what's going on: no saber-toothed tigers,

SOUTHEAST OF
LAKE TAHOE

SOUTHEAST OF
LAKE TAHOE

balen eingesammelt werden. Und außerdem ist das hier ja der Extraterrestrial Highway. Wer weiß schon, was hier draußen auf dich zufährt. Du musst grinsen. Setzt den Blinker nach rechts und zeigst dich von deiner besten Seite. Schließlich haben die beiden mehr Angst vor dir als du vor ihnen.

Und gerade als ihr da hilfsbereit, lachend und erleichtert im Nirgendwo steht, ist plötzlich dieses hohle, metallische Rauschen zu hören. Wie entfernter Donner, nur langgezogen und entsetzlich schnell anschwellend, ein martialisches Dröhnen. Irgendetwas in dir will sich zu Boden werfen, den Kopf unter die Arme klemmen und in Deckung gehen, so gut das hier geht. Aber du drehst dich langsam in die Richtung des Geräuschs, siehst die beiden Pfeilspitzen dicht über dem Wüstenboden heranfliegen. Explosionsartig schnell. Im nächsten Moment sind die Jets über euch, schlagen kurz vorher noch einen lässigen Haken und sie sind so dicht über dem Boden, dass du die grünen Helme und Masken der Männer im Cockpit siehst. Die Schallwelle trifft deinen Magen, deine Trommelfelle, deinen Schädel. Das ganze Tal verschwindet in Lautstärke. Dann sind sie weg. Irgendwer meint, er hätte keine Kennzeichnung der Flugobjekte gesehen. Und das seien keine Masken gewesen, sondern Gesichter. Grün, starrend und furchtbar. Eins der beiden Mädels kichert nervös. Wir nehmen sie mit bis Tonopah. 100 Meilen weit zur nächsten Tankstelle.

Dann fahren wir nach Coaldale. 40 Meilen weit. Eine weitere Stunde bis Hawthorne und vorbei am Walker-Salzsee. Hinter Yerington geht es 30 Meilen nach Norden, dann 35 Meilen in Richtung Südwest. Beinahe hättest du aufgehört zu zählen. Aber jetzt liegt Nevada hinter dir. Der Lake Tahoe vor dir. Hallo, Kalifornien.

no Martians, no one from Alpha Centauri or further, just two women. One next to the car waving energetically, the other timidly standing a few feet away. Probably watched too many thrillers in which naive, young hitchhikers are nabbed by cannibals out in the desert. And, after all, this is the Extraterrestrial Highway. Who knows what'll approach you here. You have to smile. You flick the right blinker and are on your best behavior. After all, the two are more afraid of you than you are of them. And as you stand there helpful, laughing, and relieved in the middle of nowhere, suddenly you hear a hollow, metallic sound. Like distant thunder, only long, drawn out and quickly rising to a crescendo; a martial roar. Something tells you to drop to the ground, with arms over your head and take cover as best you can. But you slowly turn in the direction of the sound and see two arrowheads approaching just above the desert floor. Explodingly fast. The next second the jets are over you, veering at the last minute, so close to the ground that you see the green helmets and masks of the men in the cockpit. The sound wave hits your stomach, your eardrums, your skull. The whole valley reverberates in full volume. Then they're gone. Someone mentions they couldn't identify the flying objects. And it wasn't masks they saw but faces; green, staring and terrifying. One of the girls giggles nervously. We give them a lift to Tonopah; to the nearest gas station 100 miles further on.

We continue to Coaldale, 40 miles ahead. Another hour to Hawthorne and past Walker Lake. After Yerington another 30 miles northwards, then 35 miles towards the southwest. You've almost stopped counting. But now Nevada is behind you. Lake Tahoe lies in front of you. Hello California.

HOTEL & RESTAURANT

THE COACHMAN HOTEL
4100 PINE BLVD, SOUTH LAKE TAHOE
CA 96150, USA
PHONE +1 530-545-6460
WWW.COACHMANTAHOE.COM

BASECAMP HOTEL
4143 CEDAR AVE,
SOUTH LAKE TAHOE, CA 96150
PHONE: +1 530 208 0180
WWW. BASECAMPTAHOESOUTH.COM

MODENA LAKE TAHOE

Die vierte Etappe unserer Durchquerung des Westens der USA könnte bei Freunden gepflegten Kurvensurfens auf den ersten Blick starke Abstoßungsreaktionen auslösen: Quer durch das Große Becken führend, das weite und monotone Innere Nevadas, scheint hier auf gut 530 Meilen für Fahrspaß-Liebhaber kaum etwas zu holen zu sein. Und dieses Urteil muss bis auf wenige Meilen exakt so bestätigt werden. Es sei denn, man schafft den Wechsel zu einer transzendenteren Fortbewegungsweise, die weniger den glorreichen Moment der Kurve an-strebt, als das versunkene Gleiten in einer anderen Welt. Dann findet man hier wirklich eine vollkommen se-hens- und fahrenswerte Etappe, die im Nachhinein vielleicht sogar die intensivsten Momente entfaltet: Ab der Grenze von Utah nach Nevada rollen wir geradeaus nach Osten, um bei Crystal Springs auf den Extraterrestrial Highway über Rachel nach Warm Springs abzubiegen. Hier geht es weiter bis nach Tonopah zum Highway 95, dem wir ab Coaldale nach Nordwesten folgen. Über Hawthorne und Yerington fahren wir weiter bis zur 50, ab hier sind es nur noch wenige Meilen nach Carson City. Die Grenze zum US-Bundesstaat California verläuft quer durch den Lake Tahoe – dem Ende der vierten und Start der letzten Etappe.

—

The fourth leg of our traverse of America's West could very well evoke a strong rejection response from friends of sophisticated curve surfing: Crossing the 530 miles of the Great Basin, the wide and monotonous interior of Ne-vada, doesn't seem to offer a lot for those wanting driving pleasure. And, except for just a few miles, this obser-vation is precisely correct. Unless one manages the transition to a more transcendental mode of travelling that is less about the glorious moment of the curves and more about the rapt glide into another world. Then, you'll discover a truly scenic and drive-worthy stage, which in hindsight offered perhaps even the most intense mo-ments: From the Utah border to Nevada we roll due east, at Crystal Springs taking the Extraterrestrial Highway over Rachel to Warm Springs. From here we continue through Tonopah onto Highway 95, which we follow from Coaldale to the northwest. Passing through Hawthorne and Yerington, we continue to the 50, from here it's just a few miles to Carson City. The border of the US state of California runs straight through Lake Tahoe – the end of the fourth and the start of our final leg.

800 KM • 1,5 TAGE // 498 MILES • 1,5 DAYS

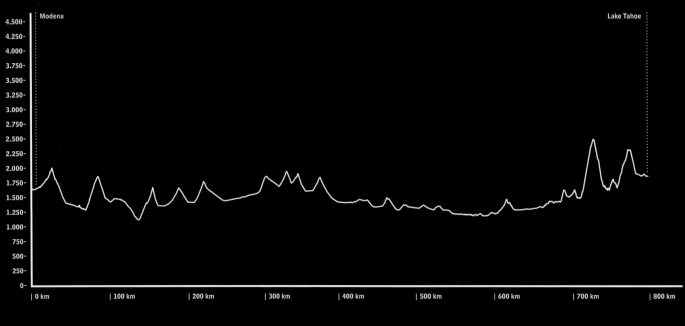

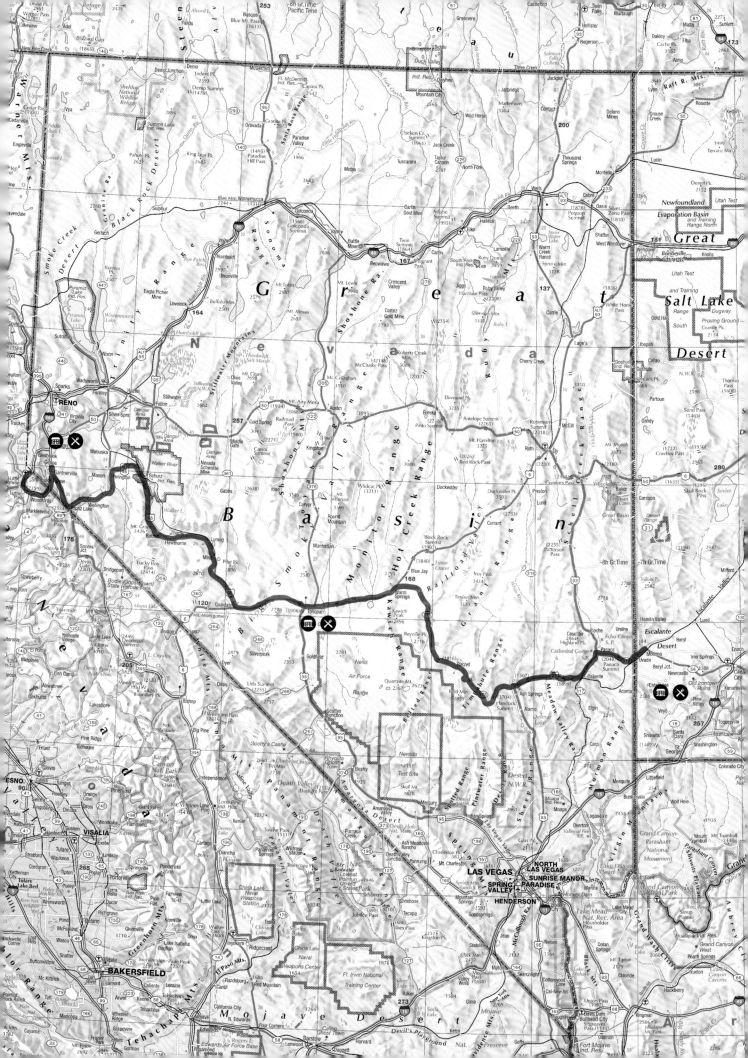

LAKE TAHOE

LAKE TAHOE
SAN FRANCISCO

600 KM • 1 TAG // 372 MILES • 1 DAY

Da draußen ist über Nacht etwas geschehen. Genesis 1, Vers 11. Gott sprach: Die Erde lasse junges Grün sprießen. Und so geschah es. Aber du hast das nicht mitbekommen. Es war bereits dunkel, als du hinter Carson City den Lake Tahoe erreicht hast. Dass die Luft feucht und fruchtbar schien, ganz anders als auf den vielen hundert Meilen davor, fällt dir erst jetzt auf.

—

Outside, something happened overnight. Genesis 1, Verse 11. And God said: Let the earth bring forth grass. And it was so. But you weren't aware of it. It was already dark by the time you reached Lake Tahoe after Carson City. Only now do you realize that the air smells humid and fecund, nothing like the previous hundreds of miles.

Beim Blick aus dem Fenster auf würzig duftende Rotzedern, auf mürben Waldboden, auf eine üppig grüne Welt, in der Sonnenstrahlen Flutlicht für Insekten und Vögel sind. Ganz langsam und andächtig ziehst du die Tür der Blockhütte auf, dann sinkst du in den Schaukelstuhl auf der kleinen Terrasse. Legst die Beine hoch und blinzelst in den Morgen. Man könnte jetzt ja etwas traurig sein, denn heute geht es auf die letzte Etappe der Reise durch den US-amerikanischen Westen. Vom Lake Tahoe bis nach San Francisco. Aber da ist keine Traurigkeit, nur unbändige Freude. Dieses Land ist voller Versprechungen und Abenteuer, der Abschluss bis hinunter zum Pazifik wird spannend, vielfältig und atemlos.

In schwungvollem Bogen schnürt dein Auto am Nordufer des Sees entlang, ganz langsam über die Grenze nach Kalifornien in Crystal Bay und dann weiter nach Süden. Immer am Ufer entlang. Es ist viel los hier oben, im Osten der Sierra Nevada, aber irgendwie schafft es der Wald rund um den See, die Wohngebiete zu verstecken. Unten in Chambers Lodge könnte ein erstes Abenteuer auf uns warten, aber wir haben vermutlich das falsche Auto: Für die rund 40 Kilometer des Rubicon Trail durch den Eldorado National Forest brauchst du hartes Material. Denn diese Strecke – eine alte Poststraße nach Georgetown im Westen – nimmt, ohne zu geben. Es beginnt mit Steinen in feinem Sand und hier glaubst du noch, dass alles gut gehen könnte. Dann kommen die Granitplatten oben auf dem Plateau mit ihren Felsstufen und jetzt kratzt bereits alles. Wenn du es aber erst einmal auf die halsbrecherisch steilen Abfahrten zum Loon Lake geschafft hast, ist dir klar, dass es jetzt kein Zurück mehr gibt. Hier könntest du ein Auto Felswände hinunterwerfen und mit weniger Materialschaden aus dem Gebüsch kratzen als eine kontrollierte Fahrt über die mannsgroßen Brocken, verblockten Passagen und fast senkrechten Abstürze ihn verursachen würde. Wir lassen das heute. Aber wer weiß schon, ob wir nicht eines Tages das Abenteuer angehen. Reckless driving statt soulful driving.

Im Süden des Lake Tahoe angekommen, steuern wir nach Alpine Village und auf der State Road 89 weiter nach Süden. Dies ist

The view outside the window is dusky-scented redwoods on an earthy forest floor, a lush green world pierced by sunrays, buzzing with insects and birds. Slowly and reverently, you open the door of the log cabin and sink into the rocking chair on the small porch. With legs raised and ankles crossed, you squint in the morning light. One could feel a little melancholy right now, because today we start the last leg of our journey through America's West. Today's trip takes us from Lake Tahoe to San Francisco. But there is no sadness, only irrepressible joy. This land is full of promise and adventure, the final stint down to the Pacific will be exciting, diverse and breathless.

In wide bows, our car sweeps along the northern shore of the lake, very leisurely over the border to California at Crystal Bay and then on to the south; tracing the shore the whole way. It's busy around here in the east of the Sierra Nevada, but somehow the forest around the lake hides the residential areas. Down at Chambers Lodge, the first adventure could await us, but we probably have the wrong car: for the 40 or so kilometers of the Rubicon Trail through the Eldorado National Forest you would need robust material. This route, an old postal road to Georgetown in the west, takes without giving. It begins with stones buried in fine sand and at this point one still believes it'll all turn out okay. Then the granite slabs on top of a plateau appear with a series of rock ledges, graunching and scratching. But once you've made it to the nail-bitingly steep descent to Loon Lake, you realize there is no turning back. Here, you could throw a car down a rock face, collect the remains from the bushes at the bottom, and sustain less damage than a controlled drive over man-sized boulders, staircase obstacles and almost vertical drops would cause. We decide against this today. But who knows, maybe one day we'll return to tackle this adventure. Reckless driving instead of soulful driving.

Arriving at the southern shore of Lake Tahoe we turn onto the State Road 89 after Alpine Valley and continue to the south. This is the Alpine State Highway

der Alpine State Highway und wir können unser Glück kaum fassen. In wilden Kurven schlängelt sich ein schmales Asphaltband zwischen Felsen und steil abfallenden Berghängen durch das Gebirge, bis hinauf zum Ebbetts Pass und weiter. Auf kurvige Passagen folgen verträumte Abschnitte, die mit sanftem Schwung durch den Bergwald ziehen, immer weiter, immer ruhiger. Dann plötzlich ist auch der Wald nur noch eine Erinnerung, es bleiben uns sanfte Hügel und eine ungezwungen dahinströmende Straße. Gute Unterhaltung, jugendfrei und family style, ganz ohne Aufreger. So muss sich die Straße nach Hause anfühlen. Es duftet schon beinahe nach Marshmellows auf Süßkartoffeln, einem mächtigen Truthahn im Bratrohr und vor allem nach seiner unwiderstehlichen Füllung. Viele Meilen später ist die schwingende Brandung der Sierra Nevada verebbt und wir erreichen südlich von Stockton das Flusstal des San Joaquin River. Der hat es wie wir aus den Bergen der Sierra Nevada hier herunter geschafft und muss nun in der Welt der Menschen Millionen Liter Wasser für die Bewässerung riesiger Felder und Plantagen hergeben, bevor er es bei Antioch in die Suisun Bay schafft, von dort in die Bucht von San Pablo und San Francisco und endlich ins Meer.

Einige wenige Meilen weit fahren wir auf den Interstates 5, 205 und 580, machen so mit der Umrundung von Tracy kurzen Prozess, ziehen an Altamont vorbei und nehmen dann die CA-84 in Richtung Fremont als Ouvertüre zu einem rotzfrechen Umweg: Die Calaveras Road zum gleichnamigen Stausee liegt nur wenige Minuten über den Städten der Bay Area, wirkt aber wie eine letzte kurvige Erinnerung an die Straßen der Rockies. Bei Milpitas ist Schluss mit lustig. Auch wenn wir jetzt am legendären Highway 101 angekommen sind, der hier in direkter Nachbarschaft zu Apple, Google und Co. fast schüchtern vorbeizieht, in ein paar Minuten oben in San Francisco ist und danach ganz erleichtert weiter nach Norden ziehen darf. Auf dem Weg nach Seattle. Er wird den Pazifik sehen. Den Blas der Wale. Das Anstürmen der Redwood Wälder an eine wilde Küste. Die Sanddünen Oregons. Sümpfe, die sich bis zum Ozean ziehen. Einsame Städtchen im Nebel der Küste.

and we can hardly believe our luck. In wild curves, a narrow strip of blacktop meanders between rocks and steep slopes through the mountains, up to Ebbetts Pass and on. The sinuous sections turn into dreamlike passages that gently sweep through the mountain forest, on and on, quieter and quieter. Suddenly the forest is but a memory, and we're left with rolling hills and a flowing, easy road. Great entertainment, G-rated, fit for family viewing, totally without drama. This is how the road home should feel. It smells almost like marshmallows on sweet potatoes, a giant turkey roasting in the oven and, above all, an irresistible stuffing. Many miles later, the rolling surf of the Sierra Nevada has subsided and we reach the river valley of the San Joaquin River south of Stockton. Like us, the river has made it down here from the mountains of the Sierra Nevada and now must supply millions of gallons of water to irrigate vast fields and plantations in the human world before emptying into Suisun Bay near Antioch, and from there into the bay of San Pablo and San Francisco and finally into the ocean.

For a few miles we drive on the Interstates 5, 205 and 580, thus quickly circumnavigating Tracy, passing Altamont and turning onto the CA-84 in the direction of Fremont as an overture to a cheeky detour: Calaveras Road with its reservoir of the same name lies just a few minutes away above the cities of the Bay Area, but evokes a last, curvy memory of the roads in the Rockies. At Milpitas the fun is over. Although we're now on the legendary Highway 101, which almost sheepishly passes the vicinity of Apple, Google and Co., and touches San Francisco a few minutes later, it's very relieved to be allowed to continue further north. On the way to Seattle, it will see the Pacific. The misty blow of the whales. The rush of redwood forests on a wild coastline. The sand dunes of Oregon. Wetlands that stretch to the ocean. Lonely towns swallowed in coastal fog. We trace its course and feel envious. We're now heading south towards San José on the Interstate 280 and then we've arrived at our final destination: Fisherman's Wharf, San Francisco. But it doesn't have to end like this.

HOTEL & RESTAURANT

BEACH STREET INN AND SUITES
125 BEACH ST, SANTA CRUZ
CA 95060
PHONE: +1 831-423-3031
WWW.BEACHSTREETINN.COM

DREAM INN SANTA CRUZ
175 W CLIFF DR, SANTA CRUZ
CA 95060
PHONE +1 831-740-8069
WWW.DREAMINNSANTACRUZ.COM

WORTH A VISIT: CANEPA

**CANEPA
WORKSHOP & MUSEUM
4900 SCOTTS VALLEY DRIVE
SCOTTS VALLEY,
CA. 95066
WWW.CANEPA.COM**

Autos, Motorräder und Trucks haben Bruce Canepa seit seiner Kindheit fasziniert. Geboren und aufgewachsen ist er in Santa Cruz, Kalifornien, wo er seine jungen Jahre mit Automodellbau, Dirtbikes und Go-Karts verbrachte. Im Alter von zwölf hatte ihm sein Vater beigebracht, fast alles zu fahren: von seinem ersten Auto, einem Ford Modell „A" aus dem Jahr 1929, bis hin zu einem fünfachsigen Diesel-Lkw. Bruce arbeitete jede freie Minute im Autohaus der Familie und sammelte Erfahrung in den Bereichen Mechanik, Fertigung, Karosserie und Lack. Heute ist er leidenschaftlich in alle Aspekte seines Unternehmens involviert, von der Fahrzeugkonstruktion und -entwicklung über den Verkauf von historischen Fahrzeugen und Sammlerautos bis hin zu Restaurierung und Rennsport. Seit 1980 sitzt Bruce nicht nur am Steuer von leistungsstarken Rennwagen, sondern leitet auch die erfolgreichen Unternehmen Canepa und Concept Transporters. Canepa ist ein sehr bodenständiger CEO und vereint Geschäftssinn, Rennerfahrung mit einer Liebe zum Detail, die ihm seinen weltweiten Ruf für Qualität, Leistung und Stil eingebracht haben.

Bruce Canepa has been fascinated with automobiles, motorcycles, and trucks since his childhood. Born and raised in Santa Cruz California, he grew up building model cars and racing dirt bikes and go-karts. By age twelve, his father had taught him how to drive almost everything; from his first car, a 1929 Model „A" Ford, to a ten-wheel diesel truck.

He worked in the family dealership every spare moment, learning mechanical, fabrication, body and paint. Today he is passionately involved in all aspects of his companies, from vehicle design and development to historical/collector car sales, restoration and racing.

Since 1980 Bruce has not only piloted powerful racecars, but also his own successful automotive companies, Canepa and Concept Transporters. Bruce is very much a hands-on CEO; combining his business acumen, racing intensity, and a focus on detail that has garnered him a worldwide reputation of quality, performance, and style.

HIGHWAY 101

Der 101 hat uns auf eine Idee gebracht. Man soll nie aufhören, wenn es am schönsten ist. Und deshalb schleichen wir uns auf der 17 aus der Stadt. Fliegen über die Berge, während auf unserer linken Seite die Nachmittagssonne kraftstrotzend über die Hügelketten der Santa Cruz Mountains flutet.

Wir schauen ihm nach und sind neidisch. Für uns wird es nun auf der Interstate 280 nach San José gehen und dann haben wir unser Ziel erreicht. Ausrollen an Fishermans Wharf, San Francisco.

Aber das muss ja auch nicht sein. Der 101 hat uns auf eine Idee gebracht. Man soll nie aufhören, wenn es am schönsten ist. Und deshalb schleichen wir uns auf der 17 aus der Stadt. Fliegen über die Berge, während auf unserer linken Seite die Nachmittagssonne kraftstrotzend über die Hügelketten der Santa Cruz Mountains flutet. Ein ganz klein wenig bekommen wir jetzt Herzklopfen, denn was wir gerade tun, ist nichts weniger als ein kompletter Wechsel der Welten. Vom rauen Inneren des Westens trauen wir uns an die sinnliche Küste, das heißt: Flip-Flops statt Wanderstiefel, Westcoast-Rap statt John Denver, Vollgas-Hedonismus statt einfaches Leben.

Die Küste bei Santa Cruz trifft uns wie eine Konfettibombe: bunt, lärmig, sexy. Bikinis und Boardshorts scheinen plötzlich Standard-Dresscode zu sein, die Welt schlenzt auf langen Cruiser-Skateboards über die Gehwege. In erfreuter Schockstarre, debil grinsend wie Teenager auf dem Weg zur Schulabschluss-Party, cruisen wir am Meer entlang. Freuen uns über die salzige Gischt, die bald einen weißlichen Film auf den Autolack legen wird und über den Geruch des Meeres, das zur Linken schäumt und donnert. Wir bummeln den Highway 1 nach Norden, steigen immer wieder aus und klettern auf versteckten Pfaden hinunter zum Strand. Sitzen dann auf dem feuchten Sand, die Arme um die Knie geschlungen und lassen uns von einem Wind, der tausende Meilen offenes Meer hinter sich

But it doesn't have to end like this. The 101 has given us an idea. Never quit when it's at its most beautiful. And so we sneak onto the 17 and out of the city. Flying over the mountains, on our left the afternoon sun floods the hills of the Santa Cruz Mountains.

The 101 has given us an idea. Never quit when it's at its most beautiful. And so we sneak onto the 17 and out of the city. Flying over the mountains, on our left the afternoon sun floods the hills of the Santa Cruz Mountains. Ever so slightly, our pulse rate now rises. After all, what we're about to do is no less than a complete change of worlds. From the rugged interior of the West we venture to the sensual coast, which means flip-flops instead of hiking boots, west coast rap instead of John Denver, full throttle hedonism instead of the simple life.

The coast near Santa Cruz hits us like an exploding piñata: colorful, loud, sexy. Bikinis and board shorts suddenly seem to be the standard dress code; the world sashays along the sidewalks on longboards. In delighted shock and awe, grinning stupidly like teenagers on the way to a graduation party, we cruise along the ocean. We delight in the salt spray, which will soon coat our car in a white crust, and the fragrance of the foaming, thundering waves.

HOTEL & RESTAURANT

SAN FRANCISCO PROPER HOTEL
1100 MARKET STREET
SAN FRANCISCO, CA 94102
PHONE: +1 415-735-7777
WWW.PROPERHOTEL.COM

TRITON HOTEL
342 GRANT AVE, SAN FRANCISCO
CA 94108, USA
PHONE: +1 415-394-0500
WWW.HOTELTRITON.COM

hat, durchpusten. Je weiter wir nach Norden kommen, desto trüber wird der Himmel. Wolken sammeln sich, vertreiben den Sommer, lassen den typischen Sonnenuntergang Kaliforniens ausfallen und versetzen das Land der Küste in einen sentimentalen Herbstabend. Die kleinen Büsche links und rechts der Straße frösteln in unbarmherzigen Windböen, draußen auf dem Pazifik türmen sich graue Wellen. An den Surf-Spots warten Neopren-Menschen schweigend auf den perfekten Moment. Oder vielleicht auch nur darauf, dass Mut größer als Demut wird.

Hinter Half Moon Bay beginnt die Zivilisation. Ordentlich und Immobilienmakler-kontrolliert. Ab Pacifica gehören wir zu Hunderttausenden, unterwegs von A nach B. In unserem Fall: San Francisco. Vielleicht werden wir uns ja über die Golden Gate Brücke nach Norden verdrücken, bis Petaluma oder ein Stück weiter, um in einem kleinen Hotel in den Hügeln von Colorado zu träumen. Von Kurven zwischen Felsen unter einem herrlich blauen Himmel.

We meander along Highway 1 to the north, stopping often to climb out of the car and follow hidden paths down to the beach. Sitting, knees hugged to the chest, feeling the blast of a wind that has blown over thousands of miles of open ocean. The further north we go, the more overcast the sky becomes. Clouds gather, driving the summer out, canceling the famous Californian sunset and turning the land at the coast into a sentimental fall evening. The small bushes to the left and right of the road shiver in the merciless gusts that whip up the gray water of the Pacific. Wetsuit-clad surfers wait silently for the perfect wave. Or perhaps for the moment when courage overrides humility.

After Half Moon Bay civilization begins. Tidy and controlled by real estate agents. From Pacifica we become just part of the hordes traveling from A to B. In our case, San Francisco. Perhaps we'll cross the Golden Gate Bridge to the north, to Petaluma or even further, to dream of a small hotel in Colorado. Of curves between rocks under a brilliant blue sky.

SHOPPING

AETHER
489 HAYES STREET SAN FRANCISCO
CA 94102
WWW.AETHERAPPAREL.COM

BI-RITE
3692 18TH ST, SAN FRANCISCO
CA 94110
WWW.BIRITEMARKET.COM

BREAKFAST AT ELLA'S, 500 PRESIDIO AVE.

Während Dottie's in der 6th Street Nummer 28 nach wie vor das beste Frühstück in San Francisco anbietet, sind die Lage und langen Schlangen nichts für schwache Nerven. Das Ella's, seit vielen Jahren Favorit der Einheimischen, ist das entspannende Gegenmittel. *While Dottie's at 28 6th St remains the best breakfast in San Francisco, its location and the line to get in aren't for the faint of heart. The original Ella's, a longtime favorite of locals, is the relaxing antidote.*

LUNCH AT NOB HILL CAFÉ, 1152 TAYLOR ST.

Dieses gemütliche Restaurant mit seinem schmalen Ess- und Küchenbereich, der in eine ähnlich enge Weinhandlung übergeht, lässt das alte San Francisco erahnen. Die Lasagne ist immer eine Empfehlung, aber man kann auch sonst kaum etwas falsch machen. *This neighborhood restaurant is a real slice of old San Francisco, with its still-narrow dining room/kitchen spilling into what was a similarly narrow neighborhood wine shop. The lasagna is a time-honored favorite, but it's hard to go wrong here.*

CABLE CAR MUSEUM, 1201 MASON ST.

Das Cable Car Museum ist ein echtes Juwel San Franciscos, immer noch gratis und nur drei Blocks vom Nob Hill Café entfernt. Gehen Sie unter Tage, um die Rollen und Kabel im Einsatz zu sehen, bevor Sie sich über die vier GE-Motoren beugen, die San Franciscos ganz eigene Art der E-Mobilität antreiben. *The Cable Car Museum, one of San Francisco's true gems and still free to visit, is a three-block walk from Nob Hill Café. Go underground to check out the sheaves and cables at work before standing over the quartet of GE motors that power San Francisco's original e-mobility.*

DINNER AT FOREIGN CINEMA, 2534 MISSION ST.

Restaurants kommen und gehen in San Francisco, aber einige Klassiker bleiben – und das Foreign Cinema enttäuscht nie. Wenn Sie dem Dessert widerstehen können, ist Bi-Rite der Ort, um sich ein Eis zu holen – zusammen mit ein paar anderen Dingen, die Sie mit nach Hause nehmen können. *Restaurants come and go in San Francisco, but some standards remain – and Foreign Cinema never disappoints. If you can resist dessert, Bi-Rite is the place to grab ice cream –along with a few things to take home.*

WALK CRISSY FIELD, MASON ST AT JAVOWITZ ST

Parken Sie an der Bucht, nehmen Sie eine Windjacke mit und wandern Sie zur Golden Gate. Fort Point ist ein tolles Ziel, denn diese Mitte des 19. Jahrhunderts erbaute Festung ist der Grund, warum Joseph Strauss einen Bogen unter die eine Seite seiner ikonischen Brücke baute. Das alles gibt es zudem kostenlos. *Park by the bay, grab a windbreaker, and hike towards the Golden Gate. Fort Point is a worthy destination, as this mid-1800s fortress is the reason Joseph Strauss added an arch under one side of his iconic bridge. All this love remains free.*

PETE STOUT'S SAN FRANCISCO

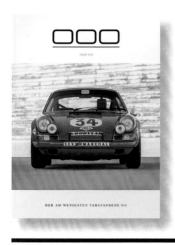

Wenn man Pete Stout und Alexander Palevsky glaubt, stand am Anfang von 000 – ausgesprochen „Triple Zero" – im Jahr 2016 eine Frage: Wie weit können wir mit einem Printprodukt gehen? Dann überschlugen sich die Dinge: Wie viele Stunden Offline-Genuss kann man als Flucht vor den unerbittlichen Bildschirmen, Hyperlinks und Drop-down-Benachrichtigungen anbieten? Das Ergebnis ist gerade in der 11. Ausgabe erschienen und eine ganz andere Art von Magazin, das sich zufällig auf Porsche konzentriert. Während jede 260-seitige Ausgabe drei Pfund wiegt und eher einem Bildband ähnelt, sagt Stout, dass sie 000 als „Magazin" bezeichnen, um nahbar zu bleiben und den lebendigen Inhalt zu reflektieren.

Mit nur 5% Werbung kann ein einzelnes Feature mehr als 80 Seiten lang sein. Rubriken können schon mal mehr als 20 Seiten umfassen, wenn sie sich mit Hahnentritt- und Pepita-Polsterung beschäftigen, frühe Fuchs-Felgen in ihrer ursprünglichen Form abbilden, Schalensitze zum Thema haben oder Porsche Diagnosegeräte mit künstlerisch wertvollen Fotos dokumentieren. Es ist alles ein bisschen durchgedreht. Aber das war schließlich das Ziel. Erfahren Sie mehr unter **www.000magazine.com**

Pete Stout and Alexander Palevsky say that 000, which is pronounced "Triple Zero," began in 2016 with a question: Just how far could they push the print experience? The follow-up came quickly:

How many hours of offline enjoyment could they provide as an escape from today's unrelenting screens, hyperlinks, and drop-down notifications? The result, now in its 11th issue, is a different kind of quarterly – one that just happens to be focused on Porsche. While each 260-page issue weighs three pounds and is more like a coffee table book, Stout says they called 000 a "magazine" to keep it approachable and to reflect its agile content.

With just 5% advertising, a single feature story in 000 can run 80+ pages. Departments can run 20+ pages as they explore houndstooth and Pepita upholstery, document early Fuchs alloy wheels in their original finishes (!), delve into shell bucket seats, or detail Porsche's system testers with high art photography. It's all a bit off the deep end. But that was, after all, the point. Learn more at **www.000magazine.com**

LAKE TAHOE SAN FRANCISCO

Auf unserem Weg vom Lake Tahoe zum Pazifik überqueren wir den Hauptkamm der Sierra Nevada auf Höhe des Stanislaus National Forest, landen bei Sonora im Hinterland der großen Küstenebene und machen uns von dort auf den Weg nach San Francisco. Um die Fahrt noch ein letztes Mal auszukosten, versuchen wir die großen Verkehrswege zu meiden und nehmen Nebenstraßen in den Santa Cruz Mountains bis an die Küste. Den Abschluss unserer Fahrt bildet dann die Route über den Highway 1 von Santa Cruz über Half Moon Bay bis San Francisco. Hier kann ein letztes Mal eine Höchstdosis Natur inhaliert werden, der kurze Abschnitt der weltberühmten Küstenstraße ist ideal für den langsamen Entzug nach den riesigen Berg- und Wüstenetappen der letzten Tage.

—

On our way from Lake Tahoe to the Pacific we cross the main ridge of the Sierra Nevada via the Stanislaus National Forest, ending up near Sonora in the hinterland of the large coastal plain, and make our way from there to San Francisco. To savor the final drive, we try to avoid the major traffic routes and take side roads through the Santa Cruz Mountains to the coast. To conclude our journey we then take Highway 1 from Santa Cruz over Half Moon Bay to San Francisco. Here, for one last time, we inhale a good whiff of nature; the short section of the world famous coastal road is perfect for the slow withdrawal after the mighty mountain and desert stages of the previous days.

600 KM • 1 TAG // 372 MILES • 1 DAY

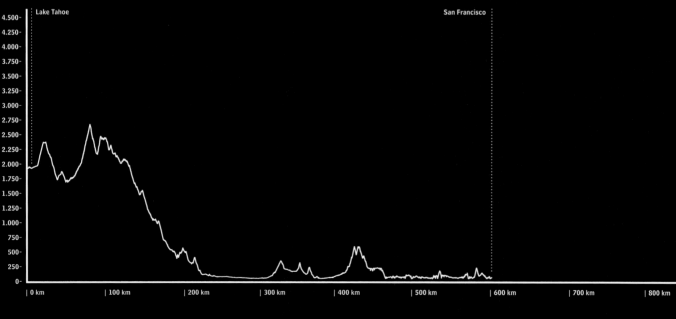

ASK A LOCAL

Der gebürtiger Kalifornier Jeff Zwart ist ein Mann mit vielen Talenten. Bekannt ist er vor allem als Fotograf, Kameramann und Regisseur, erfolgsverwöhnt ist er aber auch als leidenschaftlicher Renn- und Rallyefahrer. Besondere Spezialität: der Pikes Peak Hill Climb. Aus seiner Faszination für Porsche macht er dabei keinen Hehl – die Autos der Marke sind in seinen Fotos und Filmen überdurchschnittlich häufig präsent, während er den Pikes Peak inzwischen mit zehn verschiedenen Modellen aus dem Hause Porsche bezwungen hat. Was weniger bekannt ist: Zwart wollte eigentlich Tierarzt werden. Ein Verlust für die Veterinärmedizin, aber was für ein Gewinn für den Rest von uns.

—

Californian-born Jeff Zwart is a man of many talents. He is best known as a photographer, cameraman and director, but he is also passionate about racing and rally driving. His specialty: the Pikes Peak Hill Climb. He makes no secret of his fascination for Porsche – their cars are a common subject of his photos and films, and by now he has conquered Pikes Peak with at least ten different Porsches. Less well known is the fact that Zwart actually wanted to become a veterinarian. What a loss for veterinary medicine, but what a gain for the rest of us.

Wie sieht ein perfekter Tag für Jeff Zwart aus? Arbeit, ich mag meine Arbeit, ich mag den kreativen Prozess und ich mag es, meine Sicht auf eine Szene mit anderen Menschen zu teilen. Ich stehe gern frühmorgens auf und beobachte, wie das Licht die Welt enthüllt. Da ich meistens bewegte Bilder filme, gefällt mir, dass meine Kamera immer in Aktion ist und dass auch ich immer in Bewegung bin. Ich mag es auch, wenn die Arbeit mich an Orte bringt. Ich reise gern und sehe mir gern neue Orte mit neuen Herausforderungen an. Aber weil ich immer in Bewegung bin, kann ein perfekter Tag auch bedeuten, den Hund und meine Frau und ein ganz einfaches Auto mitzunehmen und in die Berge zu fahren.

Was läuft gerade in deinem Autoradio? Billie Eilish gehört im Moment zu meinen Favoriten, aber im Allgemeinen mag ich älteren Alternative-Rock wie The Cure, Audioslave, Foo Fighters und natürlich die Red Hot Chili Peppers.

What does a perfect day look like for Jeff Zwart? Working, I love to work, I love the creative process and I love sharing the view of what I take away from a scene with other people. I like getting up early in the morning and watching the light reveal the world. Since most everything I film is in action, I like that my camera is always in action and that I also am in action. I also love that work takes me places, I love to travel and see new places with new challenges. But because I am always in action, another perfect day is just taking the dog and my wife and some very basic car and just driving up into the mountains.

What is currently going on in your car radio?
Billie Eilish is one of my favorites right now, but generally I like older alt rock like the Cure, Audioslave, Foo Fighters and of course Red Hot Chili Peppers.

Which moment in your life do you not want to miss?
Doing things that really put your life on the line and

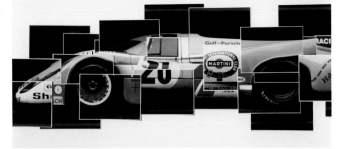

One ride and you'll understand why most rocket scientists are German.

JEFF ZWART AT LUFTGEKUEHLT MÜNCHEN
PIKES PEAK HILLCLIMB
PORSCHE AD SHOOTING

JEFF´S PORSCHE 356 IN WINTER
JEZZEBEL
PORSCHE COLLAGE
DRIVING THE 356

Welchen Moment deines Lebens möchtest Du nicht missen? Wenn man Dinge tut, bei denen man sein Leben riskiert und die einen vielleicht sogar ein wenig erschrecken, so wie der Pikes Peak Hill Climb. Momente, die viel Konzentration erfordern und bei denen man nur einen Versuch hat. Ich mag Druck.

Was ist dein Sehnsuchtsort in den USA und in der Welt? Ich hatte das Glück, fast überall in den Vereinigten Staaten filmen zu können, aber am schönsten finde ich es immer noch in Colorado. Ich war in Island, aber ich habe das Land noch nicht vollständig erkundet, also würde ich wirklich gerne zurückkehren und mehr davon sehen.

Weshalb magst du den Blick auf die Welt durch die Kameralinse? Die Kamera bestätigt mir, wo ich gewesen bin, und gibt mir gleichzeitig einen Grund, dort zu sein. Ich finde es toll, eine große, wunderbare Szene zu betrachten und sie mithilfe einer Kamera in Kunst zu verwandeln. Ich mag die handwerkliche Seite der Betrachtung, nicht nur das reine Sehen, sondern auch die Verwandlung in etwas Gegenständliches.

Wenn du nur noch einen Film sehen dürftest, welcher wäre das? „Ronin", von John Frankenheimer.

Weshalb wird ein Tiermediziner Fotograf bzw. Filmemacher? Stimmt, ich wollte Tierarzt werden, aber als mir klar wurde, dass ich Reisen, Rennsport und Fotografie verbinden könnte, fühlte sich das nach der richtigen Karriere für mich an. Es macht mir Spaß, weil ich immer noch Tiere um mich habe und gern bei unseren Hunden bin, aber ich kann die Welt bereisen, Sportwagen auf Rennstrecken und auf der Straße fotografieren und habe zu Hause tolle Hunde. Ich habe beides.

An welchen Ort der Welt, den du noch nicht besucht hast, würdest du gerne fahren? Ich bin noch nie durch Norwegen gefahren und ich mag es, wie die Straßen gleichzeitig am Wasser und in den Bergen sind. Ich glaube, ich muss bald mal nach Norwegen reisen.

Du bist ein Naturliebhaber – was macht den Reiz für dich aus? Natur ist einfach natürlich … man muss nur in sie hinausgehen. Ich mag die Veränderungen, die das Wetter und Extreme wie Schnee und Hagel und der Wechsel der Jahreszeiten bringen. Es ist immer unterhaltsam, besonders wenn man in den Bergen ist.

Was haben ein Porsche und ein Kanu gemeinsam? Sie sind beide einfach und beide Designs sind von Funktionalität geprägt. Beide sind leicht und effizient. In meiner komplexen Arbeitswelt schätze ich Dinge, die gleichzeitig spannend und unterhaltsam sind … ein alter Porsche und ein Kanu bieten beides, aber vor allem sind sie einfach.

might even scare you a bit, like racing at the Pikes Peak Hill Climb. Times that require a great deal of focus and one chance to get it right, I like pressure.

What is a longing place in the USA and in the world? I have been fortunate through my filming to have been almost everywhere in the United States, but I think what I love best is being in Colorado. I have been in Iceland, but I have not explored it fully, so I really would like to go back and see more of that country.

Why do you like the view of the world through camera lenses? To me, the camera validates where I have been and gives me a purpose to be there. I love that you can look at a big beautiful scene and through a camera you can turn it into art. I like the craft of looking at something, not just looking at it but making it into something.

If you could watch only one movie, which one would it be? "Ronin", by John Frankenheimer.

Why does a veterinarian become a photographer or filmmaker? Yes, I wanted to become a veterinarian, but once I learned that I could travel and be around racing and photograph it, I just felt that was the right career for me. It's fun now because I still have animals and love to be around our dogs, but I can travel the world and photograph high action cars on race tracks and roads, and come home to a great dog. I feel like I have both.

To which place in the world would you like to drive, which you have not visited yet? I have never driven in Norway and I love the way the roads are all around the water and in the mountains at the same time, I think I need a trip to Norway soon.

You are a nature lover – what makes the charm for you? Nature is just natural… it requires nothing other than you get out in it. I like the changes it brings you with the weather and the extremes like snow and hail and changes of seasons. It is always entertaining, especially when you get in the mountains.

What do a Porsche and a canoe have in common? They are both simple and they are both designs of functionality. They are lightweight and efficient. In my complex world of working, it's just nice to do something that is engaging and entertaining while you do it… and a vintage Porsche and a canoe are both of those things, but most importantly, they are simple.

Instagram: zwart

BAC KST AGE

„Lass uns doch mal durch den Wilden Westen fahren." Das sagt man so dahin, und dann bleiben Bilder im Unterbewusstsein zurück. Majestätische Sonnenuntergänge über der Wüste, die Felstürme des Monument Valley, Cowboy-Romantik. Dabei ist der Westen der USA viel mehr als das. Unwegsamer, verwirrender, vielfältiger. Er lässt sich nicht auf wenige Bilder reduzieren, die so auch in einer Zigarettenwerbung vorkommen könnten. Es geht los in Salt Lake City oder Denver, und selbst diese beiden Städte sind anders, als man sie erwartet hätte. Größer, dynamischer, globaler. Vor allem Denver, die Mile-High-City am Fuß der Rocky Mountains, besitzt internationales Flair. Wer also einen etwas leichteren Einstieg in den Westen haben möchte, findet hier seinen idealen Startpunkt. Wir würden ja empfehlen, vom Flughafen aus ein paar Meilen nach Osten zu fahren, hinein in die ewige Prärielandschaft der Great Plains. Am besten auf einer kleinen, staubigen Straße und dann drehen, wenn ringsum nichts als endlose Steppe ist. Ab dann darf das Kopf-Kino laufen: Du bist ein Siedler auf dem Weg nach Westen. Kennst nur Hö-

Let's drive through the Wild West. Once the suggestion is made, images linger in the subconscious mind; majestic sunsets over the desert, the rock towers of Monument Valley, cowboy romanticism. But the West of the USA is so much more: more impenetrable, more bewildering, more diverse. It cannot be reduced to images often seen in cigarette advertisements. It starts in Salt Lake City or Denver and even these two cities are different to what you might expect: larger, more dynamic, more global. Especially Denver, the Mile High City at the foot of the Rocky Mountains with its international flair. It's the ideal starting point for those preferring a slightly easier introduction to the West. We recommend driving a few miles east of the airport, into the vast prairie landscape of the Great Plains. Best on a small, dusty road and then, when everything around you is endless grasslands, turn back. From this point on a movie runs in your mind: you're a settler heading West. You've only ever heard about it and you have weeks or even months of plains behind you. The rolling waves of an ocean of grass – because plains are not

Bereut haben wir diesen Entschluss nie, denn die größte Überraschung der Rocky Mountains ist ihre Vielseitigkeit und Vielfalt. Da sind die weiten Täler, den Ebenen im Osten nicht unähnlich. Dann die enormen Berge, schiere Vertikale, und in ihrer Wildheit wunderschön.

We never regretted this decision, because the greatest surprise of the Rocky Mountains is their multifacetedness and diversity. There are the wide valleys, not unlike the plains in the east. Then the mighty mountains, rising vertically, and stunning in their savagery.

rensagen. Und hast Wochen oder gar Monate in den Plains hinter dir. Das unaufhörliche Wogen eines Ozeans aus Gras. Denn flach sind die Ebenen nicht. Nur entsetzlich zermürbend. Eine scheinbar unendliche Geschichte, eine morgendliche Wiederkehr des gestrigen Tages, eine Endlosschleife. Dann endlich siehst du die Berge, zuerst wie einen blauen Dunst, dann immer realer. Und du beginnst zu glauben, dass es diesen Westen gibt. Sein Gold und Silber, die Pelze und Reichtümer und drüben, auf der anderen Seite, das gelobte Land. Mit diesem Bild im Kopf nimmst du Anlauf und fährst los. In die Berge. Wie in einen Traum.

Genau das haben wir in unserer Version der Geschichte aber nicht getan. Sondern mit einem unerwarteten Beginn im Nordwesten, in Salt Lake City, quasi hinter den Bergen, unseren Hut vor den Rockies gezogen. Es ging uns um ein Ausloten dieses mächtigen Gebirges in alle Richtungen. Von Nord bis Süd, von Ost nach West. Bereut haben wir diesen Entschluss nie, denn die größte Überraschung der Rocky Mountains ist ihre Vielseitigkeit und Vielfalt. Da sind die weiten Täler, den Ebenen im Osten nicht unähnlich. Dann die enormen Berge, schiere Vertikale, und in ihrer Wildheit wunderschön. Da ist eine satte Vegetation und eine turbulente Tierwelt – wir hatten Elche, Hirsche und Kojoten vor uns auf der Straße, waren umgeben von Vögeln, Reptilien und Insekten, kamen aus dem Staunen kaum heraus. Nordische Schroffheit im einen Tal und beinahe mediterrane Lieblichkeit im nächsten. Regelrecht vollgepumpt mit Schönheit waren wir dann bereit für die scheinbar unbelebten Viertel Utahs und Nevadas, die roten Flussschleifen am San Juan River mit ihren versteckten Oasen. Die Mondlandschaften der Wüstengebiete. Wir allein in einem silbernen Porsche 911 Carrera 4S unter einer heißen Sonne, ringsum nichts als Einsamkeit. Das hat uns beeindruckt: Wie emotional und gelassen zugleich diese deutsche Sportwagen-Ikone in ihrer jüngsten Evolutionsstufe die vielschichtigen Etappen der langen Reise nach Westen absolviert hat. Ein Star in den Kurven und ein unfassbar geerdeter Cruiser auf den langen Geraden.

flat, only terribly exhausting. A seemingly never-ending story, every morning a rerun of the day before, an endless loop. Then, at last, you see the mountains, at first a hazy blue mirage, then more and more real. And you start to believe that "The West" actually exists. Its gold and silver, the fur and riches on the other side – the Promised Land. With this image in mind, you get wind in your sails and you take off into the mountains. As if in a dream.

But in our version of the story, this is precisely what we didn't do. We took the unexpected start in the northwest, in Salt Lake City, from virtually behind the mountains, tipping our hats to the Rockies. For us, it was about exploring this mighty mountain range in all directions: from north to south, from east to west. We never regretted this decision, because the greatest surprise of the Rocky Mountains is their multifacetedness and diversity. There are the wide valleys, not unlike the plains in the east. Then the mighty mountains, rising vertically, and stunning in their savagery. There's the lush vegetation and turbulent animal world; we saw moose, deer and coyotes on the road, we were surrounded by birds, reptiles and insects that blew our minds. Nordic ruggedness in one valley, an almost Mediterranean charm in the next. Filled to the brim with beauty, we were then ready for the seemingly lifeless parts of Utah and Nevada, the red loops of the San Juan River with their hidden oases. The moonscapes of the desert regions. Just us, alone, in a silver Porsche 911 Carrera 4S under a scorching sun, surrounded by nothing but space. This impressed us: how emotional yet relaxed this iconic German sports car of the latest generation endured the multilayered stages of the long journey to the West. A star in the corners and an incredibly grounded cruiser on the long straights. Always on, always unfiltered, despite its captivating technical perfection. Once again, we can give thanks for the chance to travel with this character actor. Thanks to Porsche. You're a dream team. Having your support is a privilege that we do not take for granted. A dusty, dry and pine-scented thank

Immer on, immer ungefiltert, trotz einer mittlerweile beste-chen-den technischen Perfektion. Wir können wieder ein-mal nur Danke sagen für die Chance, die Reise mit diesem Charakterdarsteller unternehmen zu dürfen. Danke an Porsche. Ihr seid ein Dream-Team. Euch als Unterstützer zu haben, ist ein Privileg, das wir nicht für selbstverständ-lich nehmen. Ein staubiges, trockenes und nach Pinien-wäldern duftendes Dankeschön geht raus an all die Familien und Freunde, die CURVES mitdenken und tragen. Dieses Mal waren wir ganz besonders lang und weit unterwegs, in einem Paralleluniversum gleich hinter dem Mars, und zu all dem habt ihr uns auch noch ermutigt. Danke an die Crew, ohne euch würde kein Foto geschossen, keine Se-kunde Film gedreht, kein Meter gefahren und kein Wort geschrieben werden.

Manchmal sagen wir an dieser Stelle auch unseren Lesern Dankeschön. Sie haben CURVES von Anfang an begleitet, sind mit uns sozusagen mehrmals zum Mond und zurück gefahren und wir spüren ihre Freude am „soulful driving" auf jedem Kilometer und im Nachhinein in jedem Brief, jeder E-Mail, jedem Daumen-Hoch. Dieses Mal wollen wir aber auch „Hallo" sagen: All den Lesern, die mit CURVES Wild West zum ersten Mal an Bord sind. Genau für Sie ha-ben wir dieses CURVES gemacht. Für die Träumer von den epischen Reisen. Dass dieses CURVES vielleicht von un-seren Fans aus dem muskelbetriebenen, zweirädrigen La-ger nicht so brennend erwartet wurde, nehmen wir aus-nahmsweise gern in Kauf. Wir werden zurück sein, mit einem CURVES, aus dem Schweiß und Blut tropfen, ir-gendwann, vielleicht bald schon, und es wird großartig sein. Falls wir Ihnen damit einen Floh ins Ohr setzen kön-nen: Auf dem Extraterrestrial Highway ist uns ein Reise-radler entgegengekommen, woher auch immer, nach wo-hin auch immer und vor allem: wie auch immer. Es geht also. Man kommt ganz Forrest-Gump-mäßig auf dem Rad zumindest bis zur Area 51. Für alles danach übernehmen wir keine Verantwortung. Zu guter Letzt sagen wir den Menschen Danke, die wir unterwegs getroffen haben. Un-bekannte und Bekannte. Honky-Tonk-Sally, Dreckige-La-che-Lucy, Piano-Man und all den anderen. Vor allem: Jeff Zwart mit seinem 356, dem Kajak und den vielen, tollen Geschichten sagen wir Danke für einen Roadtrip Deluxe rund um Aspen, Colorado. Canepa in Scotts Valley – Dan-keschön. Vom Rundflug in einer silbernen Cessna über die Rockies träumen wir heute noch und fragen uns, ob das wirklich passiert sein kann. Einfach so.

Wenn nämlich am Ende eines diese Reise ausgemacht hat, dann waren es wieder einmal die Menschen. Und damit haben wir auf vielen Hunderten Meilen im Wilden Wes-ten nicht gerechnet. Eigentlich ist es immer wieder die-selbe Überraschung: Dass es in CURVES nicht nur um das Unterwegssein geht, sondern auch ums Ankommen. Bei Menschen.

Eigentlich ist es immer wieder dieselbe Überraschung: Dass es in CURVES nicht nur um das Unterwegssein geht, sondern auch ums Ankommen.

Yet somehow it's always the same sur-prise: that in CURVES it's not just about the journey, it's also about arriving.

you to all the families and friends that support and follow CURVES. This time we were on the road for a long time, in a parallel universe beyond Mars. You encouraged us to do this. Thanks to the crew, without whom not one photo would have been taken, not a second of footage shot, not a meter driven and not a word written.

On this occasion we also like to thank our readers. You have accompanied CURVES from the beginning, trav-eled with us to the moon and back, so to speak, and we feel your joy in "soulful driving" over every kilometer and afterwards in every letter, every email, every thumbs up. But this time we also want to say "hi" to all the read-ers who are onboard for the first time with CURVES Wild West. You are the reason we made this CURVES. For those who dream of epic journeys. We'd like to acknowledge that this edition of CURVES is perhaps not so appealing to our muscly-thighed two-wheeled followers. Someday, maybe soon, we'll be back with a CURVES full of blood, sweat and tears and it'll be great. Just to throw an idea at you: We encountered a cycle tourist on the Extraterres-trial Highway, coming from who knows where, going to who knows where, but really, does it matter? You can get as far as Area 51 by bike... Forrest Gump-style. We take no responsibility for anything past this point. Last but not least, we'd like to thank the people we met along the way. Strangers and acquaintances. Honky Tonk Sally, Raunchy Laugh Lucy, Piano Man and all the others. In particular, thank you to Jeff Zwart with his 356, the kayak and the many great stories for a Roadtrip Deluxe around Aspen, Colorado. Many thanks to Canepa in Scotts Valley. We're still dreaming of the scenic flight in a silver Cessna over the Rockies and we're now wondering if it really happened at all. Just like that.

If there is one thing that truly made this journey memo-rable, then it was the people. And we hadn't counted on this over the many hundreds of miles in the Wild West, yet somehow it's always the same surprise: that in CURVES it's not just about the journey, it's also about ar-riving. Among people.

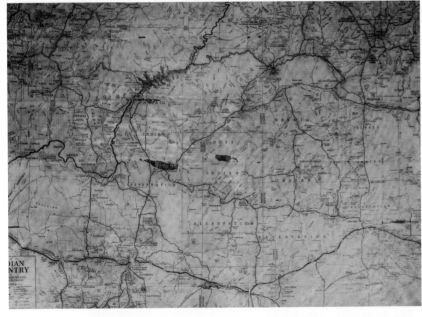

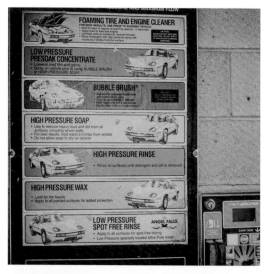

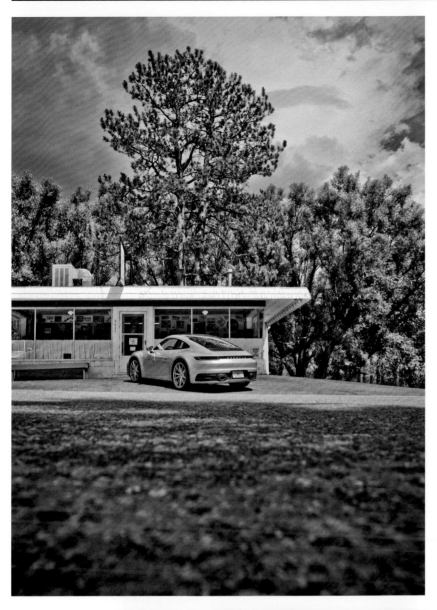

DANK AN / THANKS TO

BEN WINTER, NADJA KNEISSLER, JÖRN HEESE, AXEL GERBER, HANNO VIENKEN, MICHAEL DORN, MICHAELA BOGNER, PHILLIP HOHENTHANNER UND CHRISTIAN PREIHERR

SPECIAL FX / SPECIAL FX

BASTIAN SCHRAMM, MAXIMILIAN RAMISCH • KLAUS ZELLMER, SCOTT DEVAULT, MATT CURRAN • JEFF ZWART, BRUCE CANEPA, PETE STOUT FOR YOUR SUPPORT
TRAVIS FULTON & BARRY REINHERZ FOR THE AIRPLANERIDES, ALAN SISSON AT GATEWAY CANYONS AIR TOURS FOR THE HELIRIDE, DAVID & LOTTE!

Kraftstoffverbrauch/Emissionen* des Porsche 911 Carrera 4S / Fuel consumption*911 Carrera 4S

Kraftstoffverbrauch kombiniert: 9,0 l/100 km, CO_2-Emissionen kombiniert: 206 g/km
Combined fuel consumption in accordance with EU 6: 911 Carrera 4S: 9.0 l/100 km, CO_2 emissions: 206 g/km

* Die angegebenen Werte wurden nach dem vorgeschriebenen Messverfahren (§ 2 Nr. 5, 6, 6a Pkw-EnVKV in der jeweils geltenden Fassung) ermittelt.
* Data determined in accordance with the measurement method specified by Section 2 No. 5, 6, 6a of the German Ordinance on the Energy Consumption Labelling of Passenger Cars (PkW-EnVKV) in the version currently applicable.

CURVES TRAVEL AGENT:

AOT Travel • info@aottravel.de • Tel. +49 89 12 24 800

IMPRESSUM / IMPRINT

HERAUSGEBER/
PUBLISHER: CURVES MAGAZIN
THIERSCHSTRASSE 25
D-80538 MÜNCHEN

VERANTWORTLICH FÜR
DEN HERAUSGEBER/
RESPONSIBLE FOR
PUBLICATION:
STEFAN BOGNER

KONZEPT/CONCEPT:
STEFAN BOGNER
THIERSCHSTRASSE 25
D-80538 MÜNCHEN
SB@CURVES-MAGAZIN.COM

DELIUS KLASING
CORPORATE PUBLISHING
SIEKERWALL 21
D-33602 BIELEFELD

REDAKTION/
EDITORIAL CONTENT:
STEFAN BOGNER
BEN WINTER

ART DIRECTION, LAYOUT, FOTOS/
ART DIRECTION, LAYOUT, PHOTOS:
STEFAN BOGNER

TEXT/TEXT: BEN WINTER

TEXT INTRO/TEXT INTRO:
BASTIAN SCHRAMM

MOTIVAUSARBEITUNG
LITHOGRAPHIE/SATZ/
POST-PRODUCTION,
LITHOGRAPHY/SETTING:
MICHAEL DORN

KARTENMATERIAL/MAP MATERIAL:
MAIRDUMONT

ÜBERSETZUNG/TRANSLATION
KAYE MUELLER

PRODUKTIONSLEITUNG/
PRODUCTION MANAGEMENT:
AXEL GERBER/JÖRN HEESE

DRUCK/PRINT:
KUNST- UND WERBEDRUCK
BAD OEYNHAUSEN

AUSGEZEICHNET MIT / AWARDED WITH

DDC GOLD - DEUTSCHER DESIGNER CLUB E.V. FÜR GUTE GESTALTUNG // IF COMMUNICATION DESIGN AWARD 2012
BEST OF CORPORATE PUBLISHING // ADC BRONZE // RED DOT BEST OF THE BEST & D&AD // NOMINIERT FÜR
DEN DEUTSCHEN DESIGNPREIS 2015 // WINNER AUTOMOTIVE BRAND CONTEST 2014 // GOOD DESIGN AWARD 2014

CURVES AUSGABEN / OTHER ISSUES OF CURVES